SACRED READING

for Lent 2019

SACRED READING

for Lent 2019

Pope's Worldwide Prayer Network

AVE MARIA PRESS AVE Notre Dame, Indiana

Writing Team
Douglas Leonard
William Blazek, S.J.
Richard Buhler, S.J.

Scripture quotations are from *New Revised Standard Version Bible*, copyright © 1989 National Council of the Churches of Christ in the United States of America. Used by permission. All rights reserved.

Founded in 1865, Ave Maria Press is a ministry of the United States Province of Holy Cross.

www.avemariapress.com

Paperback: ISBN-13 978-1-59471-857-1

E-book: ISBN-13 978-1-59471-858-8

Cover and text design by David Scholtes.

Printed and bound in the United States of America.

CONTENTS

INTRODUCTION

It is with great joy that we introduce this 2019 edition of *Sacred Reading*. The Pope's Worldwide Prayer Network—known for so many decades as the Apostleship of Prayer—celebrates its 175th anniversary this year, with a special Papal Mass at St. Peter's Basilica on the Feast of the Most Sacred Heart of Jesus. Thanks be to God for our worldwide network! Thanks be to God for our apostleship!

Who could have anticipated that the Apostleship of Prayer, which began in 1844 in a house of formation for young Jesuits in the south of France, would grow into an international movement spanning ninety-eight countries and four continents? Those young Jesuits in Vals, France, were eager to serve in the foreign missions, yet they grew frustrated with the long, weary years of study and formation. It was at Mass on the Feast of St. Francis Xavier—December 3, 1844—that our founder, Fr. Francis Xavier Gautrelet, S.J., recounted how that great missionary had given his entire life to following Jesus Christ and that those celebrating his memory must do the same. The patron of the universal missions, St. Francis Xavier voyaged as far as the coast of China, passing through many trials and difficulties, entirely committed to service of the Lord. Fr. Gautrelet encouraged his charges to do likewise, not just in foreign lands but also in their own houses of religious formation. He suggested a way of being apostles and missionaries in daily life, uniting everything that they were doing throughout the day with Christ.

One hundred seventy-five years later, the Pope's Worldwide Prayer Network continues to address the challenges facing humanity and assist the mission of the Church. It is our vision, through prayer and work to meet the challenges of the world identified by the pope. His intentions are keys for our prayer and mission. We have a mission: we are apostles in daily life, walking a spiritual path called the "Way of the Heart" and working to serve Christ's mission. Along with the spirit of St. Francis Xavier, we rely on the spirit of our copatroness, St. Thérèse of Lisiuex, herself an Apostleship of Prayer member who desired to pray for the intentions of the Holy Father.

Friends, since 2010, the Apostleship of Prayer has been involved in a deep period of self-examination and, after prayer and reflection, recreated itself as the Pope's Worldwide Prayer Network. In 2015 we launched our new name and logo, and we released our updated digital prayer resources soon thereafter: these include our app, Click to Pray, and the monthly Pope Video, in which the Holy Father personally announces and explains his prayer intention. As with all change, this transformation to a twenty-first century apostolate after 175 years of deeply seated history has not been without sometimes painful growing pains. We thank all our readers and members for their cooperation, patience, and prayers.

This ministry is now a worldwide prayer network, responding to the challenges that confront humanity and the Church's mission as expressed in the pope's monthly intentions. In praying with these intentions, we extend our gaze to the whole world and enter personally into the joys and hopes, the pains and sufferings of our brothers and sisters everywhere.

The reflections in this volume are written by Doug Leonard, our former executive director, and can serve as an excellent adjunct to the Pope's Worldwide Prayer Network's practices of making a daily offering, pausing for recollection at noon, and performing self-examination in the evening. We at the Pope's Worldwide Prayer Network regional offices for Canada and the United States would especially like to thank Fr. Richard Buhler, S.J., of the Manresa Jesuit Retreat House in Convent, Louisiana, for reviewing this work.

Oremus!

Fr. William Blazek, S.J.
Regional Director
for US and Canada
Pope's Worldwide
Prayer Network

HOW TO USE THIS BOOK

In the gospel, Jesus says his disciples will fast when he, the Bridegroom, is taken from them. We know that Jesus is always with us, but during the season of Lent we honor him in a special way by entering a forty-day period of prayer, fasting, and almsgiving in preparation for the celebration of the resurrection of the Lord, Easter Sunday. The season of Lent begins on Ash Wednesday, dividing the cycle of Ordinary Time in the Church year. Sundays in Lent are not counted as fast days. Fast days continue through Holy Saturday, the day before Easter. Lent officially ends on Holy Thursday, the beginning of the Easter triduum.

The number of days of Lent corresponds to the forty days Jesus prayed and fasted in the desert before beginning his earthly ministry. Lent is a time to allow God to help us become holy, to help us look to the needs of others and minister to those needs, and most of all, to grow in faith, hope, and love, for those virtues are of God, motivating and empowering us to live the Gospel.

One of the important ways Christians observe Lent is by taking up—or practicing with greater intentionality—certain devotional or prayer practices to help them prepare to celebrate the Easter feast with greater joy. Christians throughout the world are rediscovering a powerful, ancient form of prayer known as sacred reading (*lectio divina*) that invites communion with God through scripture reading and contemplation.

What better way to deepen one's friendship with Jesus Christ, the Word of God, than by prayerfully encountering him in the daily gospel reading?

Sacred reading is a spiritual practice that, guided by the Holy Spirit, invites you to interact with the words of the daily gospel. As you read and pray this way, you may find—as many others have—that the Lord speaks to you in intimate and surprising ways. The reason for this is simple: as we open our hearts to Jesus, he opens his heart to us.

St. Paul prays beautifully for his readers:

> For this reason I bow my knees before the Father, from whom every family in heaven and on earth takes its name. I pray that, according to the riches of his glory, he may grant that you may be strengthened in your inner being with power through his Spirit, and that Christ may dwell in your hearts through faith, as you are being rooted and grounded in love. I pray that you may have the power to comprehend, with all the saints, what is the breadth and length and height and depth, and to know the love of Christ that surpasses knowledge, so that you may be filled with all the fullness of God. (Eph 3:14–19)

This book moves you through each day's gospel by prompting you at each step of lectio divina, getting you started with reading, observing, praying, listening, and resolving to act. But most important is your own response to the Word and the Spirit for that is how you will grow in your relationship with Jesus. If you are sincerely seeking God, the Holy Spirit will lead you in this process.

This book will set you on a personal prayer journey with Jesus from Ash Wednesday through the end of Holy Week. Please note that some of the readings in this booklet have been shortened for group use. The citation for shortened readings will first show the reading that is included in the book and will then show the citation for the day's complete reading in parentheses.

In prayerful reading of the daily gospels, you join your prayers with those of believers all over the world. Following the readings for Lent, you will be invited to reflect on the gospel text for the day in six simple but profound steps:

1. Know that God is present with you and ready to converse.

At all times God is everywhere, including where you are in this very moment. The human mind is incapable of fully grasping the mystery of God, but we do know some things about God from scripture. God is the transcendent ground of all being, invisible, eternal, and infinite in power. God is Love, with infinite love for you and me. God is one with and revealed through the Word, Jesus Christ, who became flesh. Through him all things were made, and by him and for him all things subsist. Jesus is the Way, the Truth, and the Life. He says that those who know him also know his Father. Through the Passion, Death, and Resurrection of Jesus, we are reconciled with God. If we believe in

Jesus Christ, we become the sons and daughters of Almighty God.

God gives us the Holy Spirit to lead us to truth and understanding. The Holy Spirit also gives us power to live obedient to the teachings of Jesus. The Holy Spirit draws us to prayer and works in us as we pray. No wonder we come into God's presence with gladness. All God's ways are good and beautiful. We can get to know God better by encountering God in the Word, which is Jesus himself.

The prompt prayer at the beginning of each day's reading is just that: a prompt, something to get you started. In fact, all the elements in the process of sacred reading are meant to prompt you to your own conversations with God. After reading the prompt, feel free to continue to pray in your own words: respond in your own way, pray in your own way, and hear God speaking to you personally. Your goal is to make sacred reading your own prayer time each day.

2. Read the gospel.

The entire Bible is the Word of God, but the gospels (Matthew, Mark, Luke, and John) specifically tell the Good News about Jesus Christ. Throughout the Church year, the daily gospel readings during Mass will come from all four gospels. The Sacred Reading series (the prayer books as well as the seasonal booklets for Advent/Christmas and Lent/Easter) concentrates on praying with the daily gospels. These readings contain the story of Jesus' life, his teachings, his works, his

Passion and Death on the Cross, his Resurrection on the third day, and his Ascension into heaven.

The gospels interpret Jesus' ministry for us. Much more, by the Holy Spirit, we can find in the gospels the very person of Jesus Christ. Prayerful reading of the daily gospel is an opportunity to draw close to the Lord: Father, Son, and Holy Spirit. As we pray with the gospels, we can be transformed by the grace of God—enlightened, strengthened, and moved. Seek to read the gospel with a complete openness to what God is saying to you. Many who pray with the gospel recommend rereading it several times.

3. Notice what you think and feel as you read the gospel.

Sacred reading can involve every faculty—mind, heart, emotions, soul, spirit, sensations, imagination, and much more—though usually not all at once. Different passages touch different keys in us. Sometimes we may laugh. Sometimes we may need to stop and worship before we continue. Sometimes we will be puzzled, amazed, stung, abashed, reminded of something lovely, or reminded of something we had wanted to forget.

Seek to feel all of your emotions as you read. Apply your intellect, too. You will confront problems of context and exegesis on a daily basis. That's okay. Sometimes you may experience very little. That's okay, too. God is at work anyway. Give yourself to the gospel and take from it what is there for you each day.

Most important, notice what in particular jumps out at you, whatever it may be. It may be a word, a phrase, a character, an image, a pattern, an emotion, a sensation—some arrow to your heart. Whatever it is, pay attention to it, because the Holy Spirit is using it to accomplish something in you.

Sometimes a particular gospel repeats during the liturgical year of the Church. To pray through the same gospel even on successive days presents no problem whatsoever to your sacred reading. St. Ignatius of Loyola, founder of the Jesuits and author of *The Spiritual Exercises*, actually recommends repeated meditation on passages of Scripture. Read in the Spirit, gospel passages have unlimited potential to reveal to us the truths we are ready to receive. For the receptive soul, the Word of God has boundless power to illuminate and transform the prayerful believer.

4. Pray as you are led for yourself and others.

Praying is just talking with God. Believe God hears you. Believe God will answer you. Believe God knows what you need even before you ask. Jesus says so in the gospels. So your conversation with God can go far beyond asking for things. You may thank, praise, worship, rejoice, mourn, explain, question, reveal your fears, seek understanding, or ask forgiveness. Your conversation with God has no limits. God is the ideal conversationalist. God wants to spend much time with you.

Being human, we can't help being self-absorbed, but praying is not just about our own needs. We are often moved by the gospel to pray for others. We will regularly remember our loved ones in prayer.

Sometimes we will be led to pray for someone who has hurt us. At other times we will be moved to pray for a class of people in need wherever they are in the world, like persecuted Christians, refugees, the mentally ill, the rich, teachers, the unborn, or the lonely.

We may also pray with the universal Church by praying for the pope's prayer intentions. Those intentions are entrusted to the Pope's Worldwide Prayer Network and are available through its website and its annual and monthly leaflets.

5. Listen to Jesus.

Jesus the Good Shepherd speaks to his own sheep, who hear his voice (see Jn 10:27). This listening is a most wonderful time in your sacred reading prayer experience. The italicized words in this passage are the words I felt impressed upon my heart as I prayed with these readings. I included them in order to help you to listen more actively for whatever it is the Lord might be saying to you.

Jesus speaks to all in the gospels, but in your *Sacred Reading* prayer experience he can now speak exclusively to you. If you can, write down what he says to you and reread his words during the day. Put all of Jesus' words to you in a folder or keep a spiritual notebook. Believers through the ages have recorded the words of Jesus to them, holy mystics and ordinary believers alike.

It takes faith to hear the voice of Jesus. This faith will grow as you practice listening. Ideally, we will learn to hear what Jesus is saying to us all day long, as we face difficult situations perhaps. Listening to the voice of Jesus is practicing the presence of God. As St. Paul said, "In him we live and move and have our being" (Acts 17:28).

St. Ignatius Loyola called this conversation with Jesus colloquy. That word simply means that two or more people are talking. St. Ignatius even urges us to include the saints in our prayer conversations. We believe in the communion of saints. If you have a patron saint, don't be afraid to talk to him or her. In her autobiography, St. Thérèse of Lisieux, who was a member of the Apostleship of Prayer, describes how she spoke often with Mary and Joseph as well as Jesus.

6. Ask God to show you how to live today.

Pope Benedict XVI commented that sacred reading is not complete without a call to action: something in our praying leads us to do something in our day. Perhaps we find an opportunity to serve, to love, to give, to lead, or to do something good for someone else. Perhaps we find occasion to repent, to forgive, to ask forgiveness, to make amends. Open your heart to anything God might want you to do. Try to keep the conversation with God going all day long.

Asking God to show you how to live is the last step of the *Sacred Reading* prayer time, but that doesn't mean you need to end it here. Keep it going. You may drift off in the presence of God, lose attention, or even fall asleep, but you can come back. God is always present with you, seeking to love you and to be loved. God is always seeking to lead us to green pastures. God is our strength, our rock, our ever-present help in time of trouble. God is full of mercy, ready to forgive us again and again. God sees us through very difficult times. God heals us. God gives his life to us constantly. God is our Maker, Father, Mother, Lover, Servant, Savior, and Friend. We know that from the gospel. He is an inexhaustible spring of blessing and holiness in our innermost selves. The sanctification of our souls is God's work, not our own.

As you read, ask the Holy Spirit to lead you in this process. With genuine faith, open yourself to respond to the Word and the Spirit, and your relationship with Jesus will continue to deepen and to grow just as the infant Jesus grew within the womb of the Blessed Mother. This in turn will lead you to share the love of Christ with all those you encounter just as the Blessed Mother draws all those who encounter her directly to her Son.

WEEK OF ASH WEDNESDAY

L ent is the ideal time to unmask temptations, to allow our hearts to beat once more in tune with the vibrant heart of Jesus. The whole of the Lenten season is imbued with this conviction, which we could say is echoed by three words offered to us in order to rekindle the heart of the believer: pause, see, and return.

Pope Francis
February 14, 2018

THE POPE'S MONTHLY PRAYER INTENTION FOR MARCH 2019

That Christian communities, especially those who are persecuted, feel that they are close to Christ and have their rights respected.

Wednesday, March 6, 2019
Ash Wednesday

Know that God is present with you and ready to converse.

"Draw me nearer to yourself in this season of Lent, Lord. Open me fully to your Word."

Read the gospel: Matthew 6:1–6, 16–18.

Jesus said, "Beware of practicing your piety before others in order to be seen by them; for then you have no reward from your Father in heaven.

"So whenever you give alms, do not sound a trumpet before you, as the hypocrites do in the synagogues and in the streets, so that they may be praised by others. Truly I tell you, they have received their reward. But when you give alms, do not let your left hand know what your right hand is doing, so that your alms may be done in secret; and your Father who sees in secret will reward you.

"And whenever you pray, do not be like the hypocrites; for they love to stand and pray in the synagogues and at the street corners, so that they may be seen by others. Truly I tell you, they have received their reward. But whenever you pray, go into your room and shut the door and pray to your Father who is in secret; and your Father who sees in secret will reward you. . . .

"And whenever you fast, do not look dismal, like the hypocrites, for they disfigure their faces so as to show others that they are fasting. Truly I tell you, they have received their reward. But when you fast, put oil on your head and wash your face, so that your fasting may be seen not by others but by your Father who is in secret; and your Father who sees in secret will reward you."

Notice what you think and feel as you read the gospel.

Jesus says to pray, fast, and do good works in secret. When we desire that others think well of us, we tend to become hypocrites; we should trust God for our reward.

Pray as you are led for yourself and others.

"Lord, help me keep secrets. Let me pray, fast, and give alms in secret today. Let me offer this all for the good of others, especially for . . ." (Continue in your own words.)

Listen to Jesus.

I love when you pray for others, as it draws you closer to my heart. What else is Jesus saying to you?

Ask God to show you how to live today.

"Lord, I start Lent with great hope. Give me grace to persevere one day at a time. Amen."

Thursday, March 7, 2019

Know that God is present with you and ready to converse.

"Jesus, you have the words of eternal life. What must I do to inherit eternal life?"

Read the gospel: Luke 9:22–25.

Jesus said, "The Son of Man must undergo great suffering, and be rejected by the elders, chief priests, and scribes, and be killed, and on the third day be raised."

Then he said to them all, "If any want to become my followers, let them deny themselves and take up their cross daily and follow me. For those who want to save their life will lose it, and those who lose their life for my sake will save it. What does it profit them if they gain the whole world, but lose or forfeit themselves?"

Notice what you think and feel as you read the gospel.

Jesus predicts his Passion, Death, and Resurrection, then urges his followers to take up their own crosses daily. If we try to save our own lives, if we hold too tightly to the things of this earth, we will lose them; but those who let go, who offer their lives for his sake will save them.

Pray as you are led for yourself and others.

"Lord, teach me your way of self-denial, for I long for eternal life with you. I give you everything, including . . ." (Continue in your own words.)

Listen to Jesus.

You have nothing to fear, beloved. As long as I am with you, you have everything you need. What else is Jesus saying to you?

Ask God to show you how to live today.

"Put me in situations today, Lord, where I can see my choice of saving or losing my life, and let me choose the way of self-denial, not for my sake but for yours. Amen."

Friday, March 8, 2019

Know that God is present with you and ready to converse.

"Father, Son, and Holy Spirit, one Lord, you are present before me in the Spirit and in the Word. I glorify you."

Read the gospel: Matthew 9:14–15.

Then the disciples of John came to Jesus, saying, "Why do we and the Pharisees fast often, but your disciples do not fast?" And Jesus said to them, "The wedding guests cannot mourn as long as the bridegroom is with them, can they? The days will come when the bridegroom is taken away from them, and then they will fast."

Notice what you think and feel as you read the gospel.

Jesus answers the question posed to him by the disciples of John: Why don't your disciples fast? Jesus' answer points to who he is: the Messiah, the Bridegroom. As wedding guests, his disciples cannot fast.

Pray as you are led for yourself and others.

"Jesus, you are always with me, yet I long to look upon your face. With that hope, let me rejoice as I fast, developing hunger for your loveliness . . ." (Continue in your own words.)

Listen to Jesus.

I am the Bridegroom who embraces you and loves you, dear one. What else is Jesus saying to you?

Ask God to show you how to live today.

"Lord, I cannot do much in my own strength and discipline. I depend upon your grace. I thank you for it, Lord. Amen."

Saturday, March 9, 2019

Know that God is present with you and ready to converse.

"Lord, Creator of All, you made humans in the image of God. You know me inside and out. Let me respond to your call."

Read the gospel: Luke 5:27–32.

After this Jesus went out and saw a tax collector named Levi, sitting at the tax booth; and he said to him, "Follow me." And he got up, left everything, and followed him.

Then Levi gave a great banquet for him in his house; and there was a large crowd of tax-collectors and others sitting at the table with them. The Pharisees and their scribes were complaining to his disciples, saying, "Why do you eat and drink with tax collectors and sinners?" Jesus answered, "Those who are well have no need of a physician, but those who are sick; I have come to call not the righteous but sinners to repentance."

Notice what you think and feel as you read the gospel.

Jesus must have known Levi's willingness of heart when he called him, for Levi simply left everything and followed him immediately. Or did Jesus speak with such authority that his invitation was irresistible?

Pray as you are led for yourself and others.

"Lord, I am a sinner. Call me. Levi became Matthew and served you well. What will you make of me? . . ." (Continue in your own words.)

Listen to Jesus.

Beloved, I will make you my lover, more than spouse, friend, sister, or brother. Our work together starts with our love for one another. What else is Jesus saying to you?

Ask God to show you how to live today.

"If I see someone I judge to be a sinner today, let me pray for him or her, knowing that you love that person and call him or her to yourself. Inspire me to speak or act in a loving way toward that person. Amen."

FIRST WEEK OF LENT

We cannot understand the works of Christ, we cannot understand Christ himself, if we do not enter his compassionate and merciful heart.

Pope Francis
February 11, 2018

Sunday, March 10, 2019
First Sunday of Lent

Know that God is present with you and ready to converse.

"Lord, here with me now, let me receive your Word, your Spirit, deep into my soul that I may stand in the hour of my temptation."

Read the gospel: Luke 4:1–13.

Jesus, full of the Holy Spirit, returned from the Jordan and was led by the Spirit in the wilderness, where for forty days he was tempted by the devil. He ate nothing at all during those days, and when they were over, he was famished. The devil said to him, "If you are the Son of God, command this stone to become a loaf of bread." Jesus answered him, "It is written, 'One does not live by bread alone.'"

Then the devil led him up and showed him in an instant all the kingdoms of the world. And the devil said to him, "To you I will give their glory and all this authority; for it has been given over to me, and I give it to anyone I please. If you, then, will worship me, it will all be yours." Jesus answered him, "It is written,

'Worship the Lord your God,
    and serve only him.'"

Then the devil took him to Jerusalem, and placed him on the pinnacle of the temple, saying to him, "If you are the Son of God, throw yourself down from here, for it is written,

> 'He will command his angels concerning you,
>   to protect you,'

and

> 'On their hands they will bear you up,
>   so that you will not dash your foot against a
>   stone.'"

Jesus answered him, "It is said, 'Do not put the Lord your God to the test.'" When the devil had finished every test, he departed from him until an opportune time.

Notice what you think and feel as you read the gospel.

Jesus resists all the temptations of the devil, out-dueling him with scripture. The devil betrays what he himself desires, but Jesus desires only to do the will of his Father. We, too, are to live by every word that proceeds from the mouth of God.

Pray as you are led for yourself and others.

"Lord, I wish to live by your Word. In your name, Jesus, give me power over these temptations in my life . . ." (Continue in your own words.)

Listen to Jesus.

I give you power, dear disciple, to do what you cannot do on your own. Receive the Holy Spirit and overcome temptation. What else is Jesus saying to you?

Ask God to show you how to live today.

"Lord, help me to replace sins and temptations with good and lovely things. Let them be my gifts to others. Amen."

Monday, March 11, 2019

Know that God is present with you and ready to converse.

"Lord, I entrust my personal salvation to you. By your Word, help me to serve you and others in my community."

Read the gospel: Matthew 25:31–40 (Mt 25:31–46).

Jesus said, "When the Son of Man comes in his glory, and all the angels with him, then he will sit on the throne of his glory. All the nations will be gathered before him, and he will separate people one from another as a shepherd separates the sheep from the goats, and he will put the sheep at his right hand and the goats at the left. Then the king will say to those at his right hand, 'Come, you that are blessed by my Father, inherit the kingdom prepared for you from the foundation of the world; for I was hungry and you gave me food, I was thirsty and you gave me something to drink, I was a stranger and you welcomed me, I was naked and you gave me clothing, I was sick and you took care of, I was in prison and you visited me.' Then the righteous will answer him, 'Lord, when was it that we saw you hungry and gave you food, or thirsty and gave you something to drink? And when was it that we saw you a stranger and welcomed you, or naked and gave you clothing? And when was it that we saw you sick or in prison and visited you?' And the king will answer them, 'Truly I tell you, just as you did it to one of the least of these who are members of my family, you did it to me.'"

Notice what you think and feel as you read the gospel.

In Jesus' prophecy of the judgment of the nations, the Son of Man will commend those persons who served the poor and needy, for he identifies with them. The Lord of Judgment will condemn those people who ignored the poor and needy. Ours is the age of redemption and grace.

Pray as you are led for yourself and others.

"Lord, what can I do to serve you in the hungry, poor, homeless, lost, or lonely? Give me eyes to see you . . ." (Continue in your own words.)

Listen to Jesus.

Your love for me will express itself in service to those who suffer. I will show you opportunities, dear disciple. What else is Jesus saying to you?

Ask God to show you how to live today.

"Lord, open my eyes and my heart to opportunities. Let me see you. Thank you. Amen."

Tuesday, March 12, 2019

Know that God is present with you and ready to converse.

"Lord, teach me to pray."

Read the gospel: Matthew 6:7–15.

Jesus said, "When you are praying, do not heap up empty phrases as the Gentiles do; for they think that they will be heard because of their many words. Do not be like them, for your Father knows what you need before you ask him.

   "Pray then in this way:

Our Father in heaven,
   hallowed be your name.
   Your kingdom come.
   Your will be done,
      on earth as it is in heaven.
   Give us this day our daily bread.
   And forgive us our debts,
      as we also have forgiven our debtors.
   And do not bring us to the time of trial,
      but rescue us from the evil one.

For if you forgive others their trespasses, your heavenly Father will also forgive you; but if you do not forgive others, neither will your Father forgive your trespasses."

Notice what you think and feel as you read the gospel.

Jesus' great prayer expresses priorities in our relationship with God and others. First we glorify the Father, seeking the kingdom, embracing God's will on earth. Then we ask for bread, the necessities of our lives. We ask God's forgiveness and offer our own forgiveness of others' sins against us. Finally we ask for endurance in difficult times and salvation from evil.

Pray as you are led for yourself and others.

"Jesus, you point out especially our need to forgive others. As I examine my heart, help me forgive these people who have hurt me . . ." (Continue in your own words.)

Listen to Jesus.

The love in your life must often take the form of mercy, my child. Do not judge others. I give you eyes of mercy. What else is Jesus saying to you?

Ask God to show you how to live today.

"Chances are that someone will offend me today, Jesus. Give me grace to forgive that person immediately. Make mercy a habit of my heart. Amen."

Wednesday, March 13, 2019

Know that God is present with you and ready to converse.

"Jesus, speak to me by your Word."

Read the gospel: Luke 11:29–32.

When the crowds were increasing, Jesus began to say, "This generation is an evil generation; it asks for a sign, but no sign will be given to it except the sign of Jonah. For just as Jonah became a sign to the people of Nineveh, so the Son of Man will be to this generation. The queen of the South will rise at the judgment with the people of this generation and condemn them, because she came from the ends of the earth to listen to the wisdom of Solomon, and see, something greater than Solomon is here! The people of Nineveh will rise up at the judgment with this generation and condemn it, because they repented at the proclamation of Jonah, and see, something greater than Jonah is here!"

Notice what you think and feel as you read the gospel.

Jesus deplores those who seek a sign from him. He likens himself to Jonah, who preached repentance; Jesus tells the crowd that he is greater than Jonah, greater even than Solomon, for he is the Son of God.

Pray as you are led for yourself and others.

"Lord, you are here. Let me repent at your command and listen to your wisdom. I open myself to understand what you are saying to me now . . ." (Continue in your own words.)

Listen to Jesus.

I am, beloved disciple, the Son of the Father. My words have the power to save you. I have some things I want you to do. What else is Jesus saying to you?

Ask God to show you how to live today.

"Although I am a sinner, I give myself to you for forgiveness, cleansing, and service today. Let me please you, Blessed Lord. Amen."

Thursday, March 14, 2019

Know that God is present with you and ready to converse.

"Gracious Father, always near me, let me pray well and learn by your Word to do your will."

Read the gospel: Matthew 7:7–12.

Jesus said, "Ask, and it will be given to you; search, and you will find; knock, and the door will be opened for you. For everyone who asks receives, and everyone who searches finds, and for everyone who knocks, the door will be opened. Is there anyone among you who, if your child asks for bread, will give a stone? Or if the child asks for a fish, will give a snake? If you then, who are evil, know how to give good gifts to your children, how much more will your Father in heaven give good things to those who ask him!

"In everything do to others as you would have them do to you; for this is the law and the prophets."

Notice what you think and feel as you read the gospel.

Jesus urges us to ask, search, and knock, requesting from God what we desire. God will give us only good things. Our job? To do to others as we would have them do to us.

Pray as you are led for yourself and others.

"Lord, focus me on what I may do for others. Let me do those things and then return to ask you for the good things I need . . ." (Continue in your own words.)

Listen to Jesus.

It is sweet to be in conversation with you, dear one. Through our intimacy, our friendship will grow into everlasting life in the kingdom of my Father. Desire that. Ask for it. What else is Jesus saying to you?

Ask God to show you how to live today.

"Help me to discern between good things and those things that only appear good. Then let me ask for the good things, Lord. Praise your holy name! Amen."

Friday, March 15, 2019

Know that God is present with you and ready to converse.

"Holy Lord, you are just. Teach me by your Word lest I sin against you or my brother or my sister."

Read the gospel: Matthew 5:20–26.

Jesus said, "For I tell you, unless your righteousness exceeds that of the scribes and Pharisees, you will never enter the kingdom of heaven.

"You have heard that it was said to those of ancient times, 'You shall not murder'; and 'whoever murders shall be liable to judgment.' But I say to you that if you are angry with a brother or sister, you will be liable to judgment; and if you insult a brother or sister, you will be liable to the council; and if you say, 'You fool,' you will be liable to the hell of fire. So when you are offering your gift at the altar, if you remember that your brother or sister has something against you, leave your gift there before the altar and go; first be reconciled to your brother or sister, and then come and offer your gift. Come to terms quickly with your accuser while you are on the way to court with him, or your accuser may hand you over to the judge, and the judge to the guard, and you will be thrown into prison. Truly I tell you, you will never get out until you have paid the last penny."

Notice what you think and feel as you read the gospel.

Jesus raises the standard set by Moses's commandments, and asks us to take the first step toward reconciliation even when the other person is angry toward us.

Pray as you are led for yourself and others.

"Lord, who in my life is angry with me, harboring grudges against me, offended by me? Lord, I pray for these . . ." (Continue in your own words.)

Listen to Jesus.

I will give you opportunities to reconcile with those with whom you need to reconcile. Be open to these opportunities so there can be healing. What else is Jesus saying to you?

Ask God to show you how to live today.

"My life is complicated, Lord. Sometimes I feel I drag my sins along with me. Give me hope and strength, Jesus. Amen."

Saturday, March 16, 2019

Know that God is present with you and ready to converse.

"Jesus, risen Lord, I listen to your Word today. "

Read the gospel: Matthew 5:43–48.

Jesus said, "You have heard that it was said, 'You shall love your neighbor and hate your enemy.' But I say to you, Love your enemies and pray for those who persecute you, so that you may be children of your Father in heaven; for he makes his sun rise on the evil and on the good, and sends rain on the righteous and on the unrighteous. For if you love those who love you, what reward do you have? Do not even the tax collectors do the same? And if you greet only your brothers and sisters, what more are you doing than others? Do not even the Gentiles do the same? Be perfect, therefore, as your heavenly Father is perfect."

Notice what you think and feel as you read the gospel.

Again Jesus raises the bar. He calls us to holiness, the very perfection of the heavenly Father. This holiness requires us to love our enemies and our persecutors, just as God does.

Pray as you are led for yourself and others.

"Lord, I am far from your holiness, but I open my heart for your enabling grace. Who is my enemy, who persecutes me? These people will I love . . ." (Continue in your own words.)

Listen to Jesus.

In humility you learn to love those who oppose you. See others with the mercy I give you. What else is Jesus saying to you?

Ask God to show you how to live today.

"Every day is a new chance to obey your Spirit and act in love. Prepare me for those moments today. Let me succeed in loving someone who hates me or hurts me. Amen."

SECOND WEEK OF LENT

Jesus did not come to bring salvation in a laboratory; he does not preach from a laboratory, detached from people. He is in the midst of the crowd! In the midst of the people! Just think that most of Jesus' public ministry took place on the streets, among the people; to preach the Gospel, to heal physical and spiritual wounds. This crowd of which the gospel often speaks is a humanity marked by suffering. It is a humanity marked by suffering, toil, and problems. It is to this poor humanity that Jesus' powerful, liberating, and renewing action is directed.

Pope Francis
February 5, 2018

Sunday, March 17, 2019
Second Sunday of Lent

Know that God is present with you and ready to converse.

"Jesus, you were God among us, and your glory was to die for us. Thank you for being with me now as I read your Word."

Read the gospel: Luke 9:28b–36.

Jesus took with him Peter and John and James, and went up on the mountain to pray. And while he was praying, the appearance of his face changed, and his clothes became dazzling white. Suddenly they saw two men, Moses and Elijah, talking to him. They appeared in glory and were speaking of his departure, which he was about to accomplish at Jerusalem. Now Peter and his companions were weighed down with sleep; but since they had stayed awake, they saw his glory and the two men who stood with him. Just as they were leaving him, Peter said to Jesus, "Master, it is good for us to be here; let us make three dwellings, one for you, one for Moses, and one for Elijah"—not knowing what he said. While he was saying this, a cloud came and overshadowed them; and they were terrified as they entered the cloud. Then from the cloud came a voice that said, "This is my Son, my Chosen; listen to him!" When the voice had spoken, Jesus was found alone. And they kept silent and in those days told no one any of the things they had seen.

Notice what you think and feel as you read the gospel.

Peter, James, and John are amazed by Jesus' trans-figuration before them and his meeting with Moses and Elijah. Then the voice from the cloud proclaims the Father's love for the Son and commands that they "listen to him." They are struck speechless by what they've seen and do not tell anyone about it until after the Resurrection.

Pray as you are led for yourself and others.

"Jesus, I believe you are the Son of God, and I put my trust in you. Will you help me do your will? . . ." (Continue in your own words.)

Listen to Jesus.

Lean on my grace, my child, for you are beloved of my Father, too. What else is Jesus saying to you?

Ask God to show you how to live today.

"If I feel your presence with me today, let me praise you and do your will. If I do not feel your presence today, let me praise you and do your will. You are Lord! Amen."

Monday, March 18, 2019

Know that God is present with you and ready to converse.

"Merciful God, I depend on you for repentance, forgiveness, and sanctification."

Read the gospel: Luke 6:36–38.

Jesus said, "Be merciful, just as your Father is merciful.

"Do not judge, and you will not be judged; do not condemn, and you will not be condemned. Forgive, and you will be forgiven; give, and it will be given to you. A good measure, pressed down, shaken together, running over, will be put into your lap; for the measure you give will be the measure you get back."

Notice what you think and feel as you read the gospel.

Jesus commands us to be merciful toward others as God is. He commands us not to judge or condemn, reminding us to forgive and be generous.

Pray as you are led for yourself and others.

"Lord, I see faults in others often. I cannot help but judge. Cleanse me of this judgmental mindset. Give me your true mercy for . . ." (Continue in your own words.)

Listen to Jesus.

I love your sincere efforts to be made new and pleasing to God. You must rely on my grace at every step. As you allow me to work holiness in you, I shall work. What else is Jesus saying to you?

Ask God to show you how to live today.

"Lord, help me to strive to avoid sin and do good today. Pick me up when I fall and put me back on your path by your grace. Amen."

Tuesday, March 19, 2019
Joseph, Husband of Mary

Know that God is present with you and ready to converse.

"Lord, you are high and lifted up in glory even as you are here with me now. I seek your guidance for my life in your Word."

Read the gospel: Matthew 1:16, 18–21, 24a.

Jacob [was] the father of Joseph the husband of Mary, of whom Jesus was born, who is called the Messiah. . . .

Now the birth of Jesus the Messiah took place in this way. When his mother Mary had been engaged to Joseph, but before they lived together, she was found to be with child from the Holy Spirit. Her husband Joseph, being a righteous man and unwilling to expose her to public disgrace, planned to dismiss her quietly. But just when he had resolved to do this, an angel of the Lord appeared to him in a dream and said, "Joseph, son of David, do not be afraid to take Mary as your wife, for the child conceived in her is from the Holy Spirit. She will bear a son, and you are to name him Jesus, for he will save his people from their sins." . . .

When Joseph awoke from sleep, he did as the angel of the Lord commanded him; he took her as his wife.

Notice what you think and feel as you read the gospel.

Joseph heard the guidance from the Lord and obeyed it, even though this guidance was counter to his culture's mores.

Pray as you are led for yourself and others.

"You guide me, Lord, to seek humble obedience that I may do your will and advance the kingdom of God in my life. Lord, I pray for humility and obedience among all who follow you . . ." (Continue in your own words.)

Listen to Jesus.

You will live in joy, my child, as you embrace the role of the obedient servant with all your heart. What else is Jesus saying to you?

Ask God to show you how to live today.

"How may I serve today, Lord? Open my eyes and heart to serving you in others. Thank you for your light, Lord. Amen."

Wednesday, March 20, 2019

Know that God is present with you and ready to converse.

"Lord, let your Word today take my mind off of me and place it on you. Let me hold you in my heart with gratitude and love."

Read the gospel: Matthew 20:17–28.

While Jesus was going up to Jerusalem, he took the twelve disciples aside by themselves, and said to them on the way, "See, we are going up to Jerusalem, and the Son of Man will be handed over to the chief priests and scribes, and they will condemn him to death; then they will hand him over to the Gentiles to be mocked and flogged and crucified; and on the third day he will be raised."

Then the mother of the sons of Zebedee came to him with her sons, and kneeling before him, she asked a favor of him. And he said to her, "What do you want?" She said to him, "Declare that these two sons of mine will sit, one at your right hand and one at your left, in your kingdom." But Jesus answered, "You do not know what you are asking. Are you able to drink the cup that I am about to drink?" They said to him, "We are able." He said to them, "You will indeed drink my cup, but to sit at my right hand and at my left, this is not mine to grant, but it is for those for whom it has been prepared by my Father."

When the ten heard it, they were angry with the two brothers. But Jesus called them to him and said, "You know that the rulers of the Gentiles lord it over them, and their great ones are tyrants over them. It will not be so among you; but whoever wishes to be great among you must be your servant, and whoever wishes to be first among you must be your slave; just as the Son of Man came not to be served but to serve, and to give his life a ransom for many."

Notice what you think and feel as you read the gospel.

The disciples don't really hear Jesus' announcement of his coming Passion, Death, and Resurrection in Jerusalem. They are caught up in their own jockeying for honor and authority. Jesus tells them that the one who would be great must be a servant, a slave, just like the Son of Man.

Pray as you are led for yourself and others.

"I give myself to you and to others today, Lord. I want to serve as you served. Give me the strength to drink from your cup, and guide me . . ." (Continue in your own words.)

Listen to Jesus.

Dearly beloved, I am here to serve you. You wish to be like me in serving others. I will show you how and give you grace to do it. What else is Jesus saying to you?

Ask God to show you how to live today.

"Lord, help me develop a servant's attitude and give me opportunities to serve. I have a new start every day in your grace. Glory to you, Lord. Amen."

Thursday, March 21, 2019

Know that God is present with you and ready to converse.

"Jesus, I live in a world of spirits. Protect me from evil in every form. Let me be with you."

Read the gospel: Luke 16:19–31.

Jesus said to the disciples, "There was a rich man who was dressed in purple and fine linen and who feasted sumptuously every day. And at his gate lay a poor man named Lazarus, covered with sores, who longed to satisfy his hunger with what fell from the rich man's table; even the dogs would come and lick his sores. The poor man died and was carried away by the angels to be with Abraham. The rich man also died and was buried. In Hades, where he was being tormented, he looked up and saw Abraham far away with Lazarus by his side. He called out, 'Father Abraham, have mercy on me, and send Lazarus to dip the tip of his finger in water and cool my tongue; for I am in agony in these flames.' But Abraham said, 'Child, remember that during your lifetime you received your good things, and Lazarus in like manner evil things; but now he is comforted here, and you are in agony. Besides all this, between you and us a great chasm has been fixed, so that those who might want to pass from here to you cannot do so, and no one can cross from there to us.' He said, 'Then, father, I beg you to send him to my father's house—for I have five brothers—that he may warn them, so that they will not also come into this place of torment.' Abraham replied, 'They have Moses and the prophets; they should listen to them.' He said, 'No, father Abraham; but if someone goes to them from the dead, they will repent.' He said to him, 'If they do not listen to Moses and the prophets, neither will they be convinced even if someone rises from the dead.'"

Notice what you think and feel as you read the gospel.

In this parable, Jesus shows that those who ignore the needs of their fellow people in this life will be judged harshly in the next life.

Pray as you are led for yourself and others.

"Lord, help me see all who are in need. Let me never be blind to those who are less fortunate . . ." (Continue in your own words.)

Listen to Jesus.

Just as I care for you, so you should care for others. In your love of them, you show your love for me. What else is Jesus saying to you?

Ask God to show you how to live today.

"Lord, your love gives me the strength to love all people. Let this knowledge inform all my interactions, Blessed Savior. Amen."

Friday, March 22, 2019

Know that God is present with you and ready to converse.

"Jesus, sometimes people do not understand you; sometimes they do and yet fail to respond. Let me understand your Word and respond."

Read the gospel: Matthew 21:33–41 (Mt 21:33–43, 45–46).

Jesus said, "Listen to another parable. There was a landowner who planted a vineyard, put a fence around it, dug a wine press in it, and built a watchtower. Then he leased it to tenants and went to another country. When the harvest time had come, he sent his slaves to the tenants to collect his produce. But the tenants seized his slaves and beat one, killed another, and stoned another. Again he sent other slaves, more than the first; and they treated them in the same way. Finally he sent his son to them, saying, 'They will respect my son.' But when the tenants saw the son, they said to themselves, 'This is the heir; come, let us kill him and get his inheritance.' So they seized him, threw him out of the vineyard, and killed him. Now when the owner of the vineyard comes, what will he do to those tenants?" They said to him, "He will put those wretches to a miserable death, and lease the vineyard to other tenants who will give him the produce at the harvest time."

Notice what you think and feel as you read the gospel.

In this parable, the tenants wish to exploit the property of the landowner. They reject all emissaries who assert the landowner's claim on the vineyard. When the landowner sends his son, they kill him. Even Jesus' audiences recognize the injustice in that.

Pray as you are led for yourself and others.

"Jesus, you know people so well. You speak so clearly to us about our nature. I come to you asking for a new nature, the one you suffered and died to give me. I ask for . . ." (Continue in your own words.)

Listen to Jesus.

I am pleased to give you what you ask for, beloved disciple. Come to me often with simple sincerity. What else is Jesus saying to you?

Ask God to show you how to live today.

"Jesus, let me work for you today, pleasing you and leaving the results to you. Let me trust in the power of acting in love even if I do not see results. Amen."

Saturday, March 23, 2019

Know that God is present with you and ready to converse.

"Father, your Son proclaimed your mercy and your greatness to the world. Give me a fresh love for you by his Word."

Read the gospel: Luke 15:11–24 (Lk 15:1–3, 11–32).

Then Jesus said, "There was a man who had two sons. The younger of them said to his father, 'Father, give me the share of the property that will belong to me.' So he divided his property between them. A few days later the younger son gathered all he had and travelled to a distant country, and there he squandered his property in dissolute living. When he had spent everything, a severe famine took place throughout that country, and he began to be in need. So he went and hired himself out to one of the citizens of that country, who sent him to his fields to feed the pigs. He would gladly have filled himself with the pods that the pigs were eating; and no one gave him anything. But when he came to himself he said, 'How many of my father's hired hands have bread enough and to spare, but here I am dying of hunger! I will get up and go to my father, and I will say to him, "Father, I have sinned against heaven and before you; I am no longer worthy to be called your son; treat me like one of your hired hands."' So he set off and went to his father. But while he was still far off, his father saw him and was filled with compassion; he ran and put his arms around him and kissed him. Then the son said to him, 'Father, I have sinned against heaven and before you; I am no longer worthy to be called your son.' But the father said to his slaves, 'Quickly, bring out a robe—the best one—and put it on him; put a ring on his finger and sandals on his feet. And get the fatted calf and kill it, and let us eat and celebrate; for this son of mine was dead and is alive again; he was lost and is found!' And they began to celebrate."

Notice what you think and feel as you read the gospel.

In this great parable, the younger son leaves home to waste time and money in self-indulgence. When he finds misery instead of freedom and pleasure, he returns repentant to his father, who welcomes him with joy.

Pray as you are led for yourself and others.

"Lord, I am a sinner, craving your mercy and love. I am aware that I deserve neither. How many ways can I praise you? . . ." (Continue in your own words.)

Listen to Jesus.

God is always good—do not forget it. Let God's mercy draw you back home. What else is Jesus saying to you?

Ask God to show you how to live today.

"Thank you for your mercy to me, Lord. Let me never forget how you have lifted me out of selfishness to depend on you and serve you all the days of my life. Amen."

THIRD WEEK OF LENT

Only God can give us true happiness: it is useless to waste our time seeking it elsewhere, in wealth, in pleasure, in power, in a career. . . . The kingdom of God is the realization of all our aspirations because at the same time, it is the salvation of mankind and the glory of God.

Pope Francis
February 18, 2018

Sunday, March 24, 2019
Third Sunday of Lent

Know that God is present with you and ready to converse.

"Jesus, I see great suffering in the world. Give me your light from your Word."

Read the gospel: Luke 13:1–9.

At that very time there were some present who told Jesus about the Galileans whose blood Pilate had mingled with their sacrifices. He asked them, "Do you think that because these Galileans suffered in this way they were worse sinners than all other Galileans? No, I tell you; but unless you repent, you will all perish as they did. Or those eighteen who were killed when the tower of Siloam fell on them—do you think that they were worse offenders than all the others living in Jerusalem? No, I tell you; but unless you repent, you will all perish just as they did."

Then he told this parable: "A man had a fig tree planted in his vineyard; and he came looking for fruit on it and found none. So he said to the gardener, 'See here! For three years I have come looking for fruit on this fig tree, and still I find none. Cut it down! Why should it be wasting the soil?' He replied, 'Sir, let it alone for one more year, until I dig round it and put manure on it. If it bears fruit next year, well and good; but if not, you can cut it down.'"

Notice what you think and feel as you read the gospel.

Jesus tells his hearers not to assume those who suffer in this life are greater sinners than those who do not. Jesus urges repentance to avoid a similar fate as the Galileans who had been killed by Pilate. In his parable about the fruitless tree, Jesus urges effort and patience, in the hope that the tree will yet bear fruit. If it doesn't bear fruit, it will be cut down. God is patient with us, but we are asked to bear fruit.

Pray as you are led for yourself and others.

"Lord, let me not judge those who suffer or attribute their suffering to you. Let me attend to myself and labor for you to bear fruit in my time. I pray now for . . ." (Continue in your own words.)

Listen to Jesus.

See, my child, I have much to teach you. I offer you the opportunity to see others with God's eyes. I love you. Reach out to those who suffer. What else is Jesus saying to you?

Ask God to show you how to live today.

"Lord, thank you for your wisdom. I resolve to obey you. Help me to reach out to those who suffer. Amen."

Monday, March 25, 2019
Annunciation of the Lord

**Know that God is present with
you and ready to converse.**

"Here am I before you, Lord, God of Hosts. Teach me
by your Word to do your will."

Read the gospel: Luke 1:26–38.

In the sixth month the angel Gabriel was sent by
God to a town in Galilee called Nazareth, to a virgin
engaged to a man whose name was Joseph, of the
house of David. The virgin's name was Mary. And he
came to her and said, "Greetings, favored one! The
Lord is with you." But she was much perplexed by his
words and pondered what sort of greeting this might
be. The angel said to her, "Do not be afraid, Mary, for
you have found favor with God. And now, you will
conceive in your womb and bear a son, and you will
name him Jesus. He will be great, and will be called
the Son of the Most High, and the Lord God will give
to him the throne of his ancestor David. He will reign
over the house of Jacob for ever, and of his kingdom
there will be no end." Mary said to the angel, "How
can this be, since I am a virgin?" The angel said to her,
"The Holy Spirit will come upon you, and the power
of the Most High will overshadow you; therefore the
child to be born will be holy; he will be called Son of
God. And now, your relative Elizabeth in her old age
has also conceived a son; and this is the sixth month
for her who was said to be barren. For nothing will be

impossible with God." Then Mary said, "Here am I, the servant of the Lord; let it be with me according to your word." Then the angel departed from her.

Notice what you think and feel as you read the gospel.

Usually in scripture people who see angels are stricken with fear, yet Mary is not afraid of the angel but perplexed by the greeting and by the prophetic message that she will be the mother of the Son of the Most High God. But her spirit is open and she says yes to the Holy Spirit.

Pray as you are led for yourself and others.

"Mary, I honor you for your willingness to be the Mother of God. I bless you. I ask your prayers, Mother, for these . . ." (Continue in your own words.)

Listen to Jesus.

I love my mother, too, and honor her as you do. She prays for you and all her children. God hears her. What else is Jesus saying to you?

Ask God to show you how to live today.

"Lord, by your grace help me to say yes to your will today. Show me that nothing is impossible with God. Amen."

Tuesday, March 26, 2019

Know that God is present with you and ready to converse.

"Father, let me eat the food your Son, Jesus Christ, gives to me. He is the Word, and he feeds me with himself."

Read the gospel: John 4:5–10, 27–42 (Jn 4:5–42).

So Jesus came to a Samaritan city called Sychar, near the plot of ground that Jacob had given to his son Joseph. Jacob's well was there, and Jesus, tired out by his journey, was sitting by the well. It was about noon.

A Samaritan woman came to draw water, and Jesus said to her, "Give me a drink." (His disciples had gone to the city to buy food.) The Samaritan woman said to him, "How is it that you, a Jew, ask a drink of me, a woman of Samaria?" (Jews do not share things in common with Samaritans.) Jesus answered her, "If you knew the gift of God, and who it is that is saying to you, 'Give me a drink,' you would have asked him, and he would have given you living water." . . .

Just then his disciples came. They were astonished that he was speaking with a woman, but no one said, "What do you want?" or, "Why are you speaking with her?" Then the woman left her water jar and went back to the city. She said to the people, "Come and see a man who told me everything I have ever done! He cannot be the Messiah, can he?" They left the city and were on their way to him.

Meanwhile the disciples were urging him, "Rabbi, eat something." But he said to them, "I have food to eat that you do not know about." So the disciples said to one another, "Surely no one has brought him something to eat?" Jesus said to them, "My food is to do the will of him who sent me and to complete his work. Do you not say, 'Four months more, then comes the harvest'? But I tell you, look around you, and see how the fields are ripe for harvesting. The reaper is already receiving wages and is gathering fruit for eternal life, so that sower and reaper may rejoice together. For here the saying holds true, 'One sows and another reaps.' I sent you to reap that for which you did not labor. Others have labored, and you have entered into their labor."

Many Samaritans from that city believed in him because of the woman's testimony, "He told me everything I have ever done." So when the Samaritans came to him, they asked him to stay with them; and he stayed there for two days. And many more believed because of his word. They said to the woman, "It is no longer because of what you said that we believe, for we have heard for ourselves, and we know that this is truly the Savior of the world."

Notice what you think and feel as you read the gospel.

Jesus is exhausted by his journey, yet instead of satiating his own hunger, he first does the will of his Father, calling sinners to return to him. Instead of slaking his own thirst, he pours out the living water for the Samaritan woman.

Pray as you are led for yourself and others.

"Lord, I too get exhausted on the journey of life. Pour out your living water for me; feed me, and all those you've given me, with a hunger for God's will . . ." (Continue in your own words.)

Listen to Jesus.

This is the journey of faith, dear disciple. Entrust yourself entirely to God, giving up your own will and seeking God's. God will work in your life and bless you. What else is Jesus saying to you?

Ask God to show you how to live today.

"Lord, I abandon all to you today. Take all of me and do with me what you will. I seek your power to do what pleases you. Amen."

Wednesday, March 27, 2019

Know that God is present with you and ready to converse.

"Lord, give me deep understanding of your commandments by your Word."

Read the gospel: Matthew 5:17–19.

Jesus said, "Do not think that I have come to abolish the law or the prophets; I have come not to abolish but to fulfill. For truly I tell you, until heaven and earth pass away, not one letter, not one stroke of a letter, will pass from the law until all is accomplished. Therefore,

whoever breaks one of the least of these commandments, and teaches others to do the same, will be called
least in the kingdom of heaven; but whoever does them
and teaches them will be called great in the kingdom
of heaven."

Notice what you think and feel as you read the gospel.

Jesus says he fulfills the law and the prophets and that
all they have said will come to pass. Those who break
the commandments will be called least in the kingdom,
especially those who teach others to break them.

Pray as you are led for yourself and others.

"Lord, let me not abuse the liberty of your law of love,
which comprises all of the law and the prophets. Let
me understand deeply that God's morality is exacting
and I am called to obedience, not for the sake of legality
but for the sake of love. Keep me from leading any of
these into error . . ." (Continue in your own words.)

Listen to Jesus.

*The proper fear of God is to guard yourself and your heart
that you may not offend God. If you sin, you may come to
the infinite forgiveness I offer. I will wash you white as snow.*
What else is Jesus saying to you?

Ask God to show you how to live today.

"Lord, I place my sinful self in your hands. Only you
can forgive and cleanse me. Give me your Spirit that

I may walk in your grace and reflect your grace upon others. Amen."

Thursday, March 28, 2019

Know that God is present with you and ready to converse.

"Lord, I live in a world full of spiritual forces. I seek only you by the Holy Spirit. Let the Spirit illuminate your Word to me."

Read the gospel: Luke 11:14–23.

Now Jesus was casting out a demon that was mute; when the demon had gone out, the one who had been mute spoke, and the crowds were amazed. But some of them said, "He casts out demons by Beelzebul, the ruler of the demons." Others, to test him, kept demanding from him a sign from heaven. But he knew what they were thinking and said to them, "Every kingdom divided against itself becomes a desert, and house falls on house. If Satan also is divided against himself, how will his kingdom stand?—for you say that I cast out the demons by Beelzebul. Now if I cast out the demons by Beelzebul, by whom do your exorcists cast them out? Therefore they will be your judges. But if it is by the finger of God that I cast out the demons, then the kingdom of God has come to you. When a strong man, fully armed, guards his castle, his property is safe. But when one stronger than he attacks him and overpowers him, he takes away his armor in which he trusted and divides his plunder. Whoever is not with

me is against me, and whoever does not gather with
me scatters."

Notice what you think and feel as you read the gospel.

Seeing his power over evil spirits, some in the crowd
accuse Jesus of being in league with Satan, Beelzebul.
Jesus repudiates that idea, pointing out that a divided
kingdom cannot stand. He describes himself as a man
stronger than the strong man, for Jesus exercises the
power of God.

Pray as you are led for yourself and others.

"Lord, protect me and those I love from evil. Vanquish
evil by your power, and let us all gather with you . . ."
(Continue in your own words.)

Listen to Jesus.

*Dearest soul, I am your protector. Sometimes you will be
opposed by powers greater than yourself. Always turn to
me, trusting me and praying for my protection, for there is
no power greater than I.* What else is Jesus saying to you?

Ask God to show you how to live today.

"Lord, if there is any evil jeopardizing me or those you
have given me, direct me to pray. Give me discernment
that I may turn to you for all rescue and protection.
Thank you, mighty Savior. Amen."

Friday, March 29, 2019

Know that God is present with you and ready to converse.

"Lord, I am here before you, hungry for your Word."

Read the gospel: Mark 12:28–34.

One of the scribes came near and heard them disputing with one another, and seeing that Jesus answered them well, he asked Jesus, "Which commandment is the first of all?" Jesus answered, "The first is, 'Hear, O Israel: the Lord our God, the Lord is one; you shall love the Lord your God with all your heart, and with all your soul, and with all your mind, and with all your strength.' The second is this, 'You shall love your neighbor as yourself.' There is no other commandment greater than these." Then the scribe said to him, "You are right, Teacher; you have truly said that 'he is one, and besides him there is no other'; and 'to love him with all the heart, and with all the understanding, and with all the strength,' and 'to love one's neighbor as oneself,'—this is much more important than all whole burnt offerings and sacrifices." When Jesus saw that he answered wisely, he said to him, "You are not far from the kingdom of God." After that no one dared to ask him any question.

Notice what you think and feel as you read the gospel.

Jesus must have loved the scribe who understood the greatest commandments of the law. Loving God and one's neighbor includes all the commandments of the law and the prophets. Jesus assures the scribe he is "not far" from the kingdom.

Pray as you are led for yourself and others.

"Lord, I embrace your law of love. Fill me with the love in your own heart. Let me love others as you loved the scribe . . ." (Continue in your own words.)

Listen to Jesus.

In love is all your power, dear disciple. Take up your cross and follow me in your journey of love. What else is Jesus saying to you?

Ask God to show you how to live today.

"Lord, if you walk with me, I can bear my cross today. Fill me with love for others so that I may love with your love. I glorify your name, Blessed Savior. Amen."

Saturday, March 30, 2019

Know that God is present with you and ready to converse.

"Lord, I seek your righteousness and your wisdom. By your Holy Word, show me how to obtain them."

Read the gospel: Luke 18:9–14.

Jesus also told this parable to some who trusted in themselves that they were righteous and regarded others with contempt: "Two men went up to the temple to pray, one a Pharisee and the other a tax collector. The

Pharisee, standing by himself, was praying thus, 'God, I thank you that I am not like other people: thieves, rogues, adulterers, or even like this tax collector. I fast twice a week; I give a tenth of all my income.' But the tax collector, standing far off, would not even look up to heaven, but was beating his breast and saying, 'God, be merciful to me, a sinner!' I tell you, this man went down to his home justified rather than the other; for all who exalt themselves will be humbled, but all who humble themselves will be exalted."

Notice what you think and feel as you read the gospel.

Jesus knows it's human nature to honor oneself. This trait makes us judge others. The sinful tax collector acknowledges his sin to God, while the Pharisee vaunts his own virtues. The tax collector, Jesus says, goes home forgiven. The Pharisee has yet to learn humility.

Pray as you are led for yourself and others.

God be merciful to me, a sinner! I pray for those who have difficulty repenting . . ." (Continue in your own words.)

Listen to Jesus.

I forgive you, beloved follower. I give you light to recognize your sins in this season. Take it to heart and seek my mercy and cleansing. This is how you grow in the Lord. What else is Jesus saying to you?

Ask God to show you how to live today.

"Lord, I praise you for the greatness of your mercy! Help me to live today both in contrition, knowing my many sins, and in joy and awe at your goodness. Amen."

FOURTH WEEK OF LENT

Jesus is our Teacher, powerful in word and deed. Jesus imparts to us all the light that illuminates the sometimes dark paths of our lives. He also transmits to us the necessary strength to overcome difficulties, trials, and temptations. Let us consider what a great grace it is for us to have known this God who is so powerful and so good! A teacher and a friend who shows us the path and takes care of us especially when we are in need.

Pope Francis
January 28, 2018

Sunday, March 31, 2019
Fourth Sunday of Lent

Know that God is present with you and ready to converse.

"Lord, I sometimes wander away from you and your love. Teach me how to return through your Word."

Read the gospel: Luke 15:11–32 (Lk 15:1–3, 11–32).

Then Jesus said, "There was a man who had two sons. The younger of them said to his father, 'Father, give me the share of the property that will belong to me.' So he divided his property between them. A few days later the younger son gathered all he had and travelled to a distant country, and there he squandered his property in dissolute living. When he had spent everything, a severe famine took place throughout that country, and he began to be in need. So he went and hired himself out to one of the citizens of that country, who sent him to his fields to feed the pigs. He would gladly have filled himself with the pods that the pigs were eating; and no one gave him anything. But when he came to himself he said, 'How many of my father's hired hands have bread enough and to spare, but here I am dying of hunger! I will get up and go to my father, and I will say to him, "Father, I have sinned against heaven and before you; I am no longer worthy to be called your son; treat me like one of your hired hands."' So he set off and went to his father. But while he was still far off, his father saw him and was filled with compassion; he ran and put his arms around him and kissed him. Then the son said to him, 'Father, I have sinned against heaven and before you; I am no longer worthy to be called your son.' But the father said to his slaves, 'Quickly, bring out a robe—the best one—and put it on him; put a ring on his finger and sandals on his feet. And get the fatted calf and kill it, and let us eat and celebrate; for this son of mine was dead and is alive again; he was lost and is found!' And they began to celebrate.

"Now his elder son was in the field; and when he came and approached the house, he heard music and dancing. He called one of the slaves and asked what was going on. He replied, 'Your brother has come, and your father has killed the fatted calf, because he has got him back safe and sound.' Then he became angry and refused to go in. His father came out and began to plead with him. But he answered his father, 'Listen! For all these years I have been working like a slave for you, and I have never disobeyed your command; yet you have never given me even a young goat so that I might celebrate with my friends. But when this son of yours came back, who has devoured your property with prostitutes, you killed the fatted calf for him!' Then the father said to him, 'Son, you are always with me, and all that is mine is yours. But we had to celebrate and rejoice, because this brother of yours was dead and has come to life; he was lost and has been found.'"

Notice what you think and feel as you read the gospel.

The Lord tells the great parable about the prodigal son. The lesson is twofold: let those brought to ruin by their sin return to the merciful Father; let those who have remained with the Father, be merciful in accepting the returning sinner.

Pray as you are led for yourself and others.

"Lord, I enter into your merciful embrace. I rejoice when others return to you. I pray for sinners to come to you now . . ." (Continue in your own words.)

Listen to Jesus.

It is my joy to open your heart, mind, and soul to me, my child. Give yourself to me every day, and I will change your life. What else is Jesus saying to you?

Ask God to show you how to live today.

"Take me by the hand, Lord, bring me back to you, and help me please you today."

THE POPE'S MONTHLY PRAYER INTENTION FOR APRIL 2019

For doctors and their humanitarian collaborators in war zones, who risk their lives to save the lives of others.

Monday, April 1, 2019

Know that God is present with you and ready to converse.

"Lord, let me find you in the darkness of the world and even within my own darkness. You are the Light of the world."

Read the gospel: John 9:1–3, 6–7, 13–41 (Jn 9:1–41).

As Jesus walked along, he saw a man blind from birth. His disciples asked him, "Rabbi, who sinned, this man or his parents, that he was born blind?" Jesus answered, "Neither this man nor his parents sinned; he was born blind so that God's works might be revealed in him." . . . When he had said this, he spat on the ground and made mud with the saliva and spread the mud on the man's eyes, saying to him, "Go, wash in the pool of Siloam"(which means Sent). Then the man went and washed and came back able to see. . . .

His neighbors brought to the Pharisees the man who had formerly been blind. Now it was a sabbath day when Jesus made the mud and opened his eyes. Then the Pharisees also began to ask him how he had received his sight. He said to them, "He put mud on my eyes. Then I washed, and now I see." Some of the Pharisees said, "This man is not from God, for he does not observe the sabbath." But others said, "How can a man who is a sinner perform such signs?" And they were divided. So they said again to the blind man, "What do you say about him? It was your eyes he opened." He said, "He is a prophet."

The Jews did not believe that he had been blind and had received his sight until they called the parents of the man who had received his sight and asked them, "Is this your son, who you say was born blind? How then does he now see?" His parents answered, "We know that this is our son, and that he was born blind; but we do not know how it is that now he sees, nor do we know who opened his eyes. Ask him; he is of age. He will speak for himself." His parents said this because they were afraid of the Jews; for the Jews had already agreed that anyone who confessed Jesus to be the Messiah would be put out of the synagogue. Therefore his parents said, "He is of age; ask him."

So for the second time they called the man who had been blind, and they said to him, "Give glory to God! We know that this man is a sinner." He answered, "I do not know whether he is a sinner. One thing I do know, that though I was blind, now I see." They said to him, "What did he do to you? How did he open your eyes?" He answered them, "I have told you already, and you would not listen. Why do you want to hear it again? Do you also want to become his disciples?" Then they reviled him, saying, "You are his disciple, but we are disciples of Moses. We know that God has spoken to Moses, but as for this man, we do not know where he comes from." The man answered, "Here is an astonishing thing! You do not know where he comes from, and yet he opened my eyes. We know that God does not listen to sinners, but he does listen to one who worships him and obeys his will. Never since the world began has it been heard that anyone opened the eyes of a person born blind. If this man were not from God, he could do nothing." They answered him, "You were born entirely in sins, and are you trying to teach us?" And they drove him out.

Jesus heard that they had driven him out, and when he found him, he said, "Do you believe in the Son of Man?" He answered, "And who is he, sir? Tell me, so that I may believe in him." Jesus said to him, "You have seen him, and the one speaking with you is he." He said, "Lord, I believe." And he worshiped him. Jesus said, "I came into this world for judgment so that those who do not see may see, and those who do see may become blind." Some of the Pharisees near him heard this and said to him, "Surely we are not blind, are we?" Jesus said to them, "If you were blind, you would not have sin. But now that you say, 'We see,' your sin remains."

Notice what you think and feel as you read the gospel.

This gospel reading is a study of human nature: all are in the dark, in different ways. The disciples don't understand Jesus. The blind man doesn't see anything. His parents can't explain his healing. The Pharisees, blinded by their theology, cannot see past the fact that Jesus breaks the Sabbath according to their laws. Meanwhile, the man restored to sight believes in Jesus, the Messiah.

Pray as you are led for yourself and others.

"Lord, though all the world be wrong, you are right. I believe in you and worship you. As we have a personal relationship, I pray the same for others, especially those in deepest darkness . . ." (Continue in your own words.)

Listen to Jesus.

I cannot do my work in those who deny their sins, beloved disciple. Turn from sin and seek forgiveness, and you will know my joy. What else is Jesus saying to you?

Ask God to show you how to live today.

"What sacrifice can I make today to show my love for you, my gratitude that you are with me, Savior? Amen."

Tuesday, April 2, 2019

**Know that God is present with
you and ready to converse.**

Lord of heaven and earth, stir up my heart to receive
your Word today.

Read the gospel: John 5:1–9a, 14–16
(Jn 5:1–16).

After this there was a festival of the Jews, and Jesus
went up to Jerusalem.

Now in Jerusalem by the Sheep Gate there is a pool,
called in Hebrew Beth-zatha, which has five porticoes.
In these lay many invalids—blind, lame, and paralyzed. One man was there who had been ill for thir-
ty-eight years. When Jesus saw him lying there and
knew that he had been there a long time, he said to
him, "Do you want to be made well?" The sick man
answered him, "Sir, I have no one to put me into the
pool when the water is stirred up; and while I am making my way, someone else steps down ahead of me."
Jesus said to him, "Stand up, take your mat and walk."
At once the man was made well, and he took up his
mat and began to walk. . . .

Later Jesus found him in the temple and said to
him, "See, you have been made well! Do not sin any-
more, so that nothing worse happens to you." The
man went away and told the Jews that it was Jesus
who had made him well. Therefore the Jews started
persecuting Jesus, because he was doing such things
on the sabbath.

Notice what you think and feel as you read the gospel.

On this Sabbath, Jesus tells the paralyzed man to take up his mat and walk, and the man does so. Some Jews tell the man that it is unlawful for him to carry his mat on the Sabbath, and these Jews start persecuting Jesus for working on the Sabbath.

Pray as you are led for yourself and others.

"How narrow is the human heart, Lord! How easily we reject your free ways of love and allow ourselves to be imprisoned by human rules and expectations. Free us from this sin . . ." (Continue in your own words.)

Listen to Jesus.

If you offer yourself to act upon my love, you, too, will meet opposition. But I will be with you, and I will work through you, dear disciple. What else is Jesus saying to you?

Ask God to show you how to live today.

"Lord, all I ask is to walk in your grace, following you, doing small acts of love. Amen."

Wednesday, April 3, 2019

Know that God is present with you and ready to converse.

"Father, in the unity of the Holy Spirit you are One with your Son, Jesus, who is the everlasting Word. Let me join you in your love."

Read the gospel: John 5:17–24 (Jn 5:17–30).

But Jesus answered them, "My Father is still working, and I also am working." For this reason the Jews were seeking all the more to kill him, because he was not only breaking the sabbath, but was also calling God his own Father, thereby making himself equal to God.

Jesus said to them, "Very truly, I tell you, the Son can do nothing on his own, but only what he sees the Father doing; for whatever the Father does, the Son does likewise. The Father loves the Son and shows him all that he himself is doing; and he will show him greater works than these, so that you will be astonished. Indeed, just as the Father raises the dead and gives them life, so also the Son gives life to whomsoever he wishes. The Father judges no one but has given all judgment to the Son, so that all may honor the Son just as they honor the Father. Anyone who does not honor the Son does not honor the Father who sent him. Very truly, I tell you, anyone who hears my word and believes him who sent me has eternal life, and does not come under judgment, but has passed from death to life."

Notice what you think and feel as you read the gospel.

Some of the Jews want to kill Jesus, not just because he breaks the Sabbath but because he makes himself equal to God by healing, forgiving, raising the dead, and proclaiming that in the end he will judge all humanity. Yet Jesus teaches that he is one with the Father; he does only the Father's will.

Pray as you are led for yourself and others.

"I can imagine how stunned people were to hear your words, Lord. You spoke the truth, but it was too much for many to take in. Open my spirit to humility to receive and believe the truth, your perfect unity with the Father, and your life-giving authority . . ." (Continue in your own words.)

Listen to Jesus.

My work of redemption is both complete and still in process. I did not come to give temporary relief to a fallen people; I came to raise all who trust in me to eternal life with God. Let me work in you, beloved. What else is Jesus saying to you?

Ask God to show you how to live today.

"Jesus, make your saving power real in me. Let me extend it by your grace and guidance to someone else today. I am grateful to you, Blessed Lord. Amen."

Thursday, April 4, 2019

Know that God is present with you and ready to converse.

"Word of God, Savior, Jesus, let me hear your voice today."

Read the gospel: John 5:31–38 (Jn 5:31–47).

Jesus said, "If I testify about myself, my testimony is not true. There is another who testifies on my behalf, and I know that his testimony to me is true. You sent messengers to John, and he testified to the truth. Not that I accept such human testimony, but I say these things so that you may be saved. He was a burning and shining lamp, and you were willing to rejoice for a while in his light. But I have a testimony greater than John's. The works that the Father has given me to complete, the very works that I am doing, testify on my behalf that the Father has sent me. And the Father who sent me has himself testified on my behalf. You have never heard his voice or seen his form, and you do not have his word abiding in you, because you do not believe him whom he has sent."

Notice what you think and feel as you read the gospel.

Jesus points out the things that identify him as the Messiah, which are not his own evidence but God's. John the Baptist, the mighty works Jesus did, and the scriptures all testify that Jesus is the Messiah. He is telling us that faith is built on the testimony of those we trust. The Jewish elders refused to trust Jesus, so they refused to accept God's own testimony, which was revealed in Jesus' powerful ministry.

Pray as you are led for yourself and others.

"Lord, you are faithful and good. In all matters, I will trust you. I entrust to you especially these . . ." (Continue in your own words.)

Listen to Jesus.

Beloved disciple, trust in me, learn from me, and I will show you the very face of God. What else is Jesus saying to you?

Ask God to show you how to live today.

"Jesus, Word of God, let my actions today bear witness to your goodness and bring you glory. Amen."

Friday, April 5, 2019

Know that God is present with you and ready to converse.

"One God, I am before you, in awe at your wonderful works in the universe, in history, in the salvation of your people. Teach me by your Word."

Read the gospel: John 7:1–2, 10, 25–30.

After this Jesus went about in Galilee. He did not wish to go about in Judea because the Jews were looking for an opportunity to kill him. Now the Jewish festival of Booths was near. . . .

But after his brothers had gone to the festival, then he also went, not publicly but as it were in secret. . . .

Now some of the people of Jerusalem were saying, "Is not this the man whom they are trying to kill? And here he is, speaking openly, but they say nothing to him! Can it be that the authorities really know that this is the Messiah? Yet we know where this man is from; but when the Messiah comes, no one will know where he is from." Then Jesus cried out as he was teaching in the temple, "You know me, and you know where

I am from. I have not come on my own. But the one who sent me is true, and you do not know him. I know him, because I am from him, and he sent me." Then they tried to arrest him, but no one laid hands on him, because his hour had not yet come.

Notice what you think and feel as you read the gospel.

As the people of Jerusalem speculate on Jesus' identity as the Messiah, Jesus states in the temple that he has been sent by God, whom they do not know. Jesus is fearless, confident in and surrendered to the will of God, who sent him. They try to arrest him but cannot, because it is God's will that Jesus should continue his ministry at this time; Jesus' arrest will come later.

Pray as you are led for yourself and others.

"Lord, I, too, give myself to your timing and the events you have destined in my life. Let me be true to you and embrace your will . . ." (Continue in your own words.)

Listen to Jesus.

It was my glory to be crucified in shame before men and women, as I did it for love. My Cross is also your glory, dear disciple. Take up your own cross in love and follow me to glory. What else is Jesus saying to you?

Ask God to show you how to live today.

"Let me make a small or great sacrifice in love today, Lord. Let it be to glorify you. I praise the way of the Cross, Jesus. Thank you for teaching me. Amen."

Saturday, April 6, 2019

Know that God is present with you and ready to converse.

"Lord, as I come into your presence let all doubt and disputation die in me, and let me receive the truth of your Word."

Read the gospel: John 7:40–53.

When they heard Jesus' words, some in the crowd said, "This is really the prophet." Others said, "This is the Messiah." But some asked, "Surely the Messiah does not come from Galilee, does he? Has not the scripture said that the Messiah is descended from David and comes from Bethlehem, the village where David lived?" So there was a division in the crowd because of him. Some of them wanted to arrest him, but no one laid hands on him.

Then the temple police went back to the chief priests and Pharisees, who asked them, "Why did you not arrest him?" The police answered, "Never has anyone spoken like this!" Then the Pharisees replied, "Surely you have not been deceived too, have you? Has any one of the authorities or of the Pharisees believed in him? But this crowd, which does not know the law— they are accursed." Nicodemus, who had gone to Jesus before, and who was one of them, asked, "Our law does not judge people without first giving them a hearing to find out what they are doing, does it?" They replied, "Surely you are not also from Galilee, are you? Search and you will see that no prophet is to arise from Galilee."

Notice what you think and feel as you read the gospel.

The people of Jerusalem speak from partial knowledge, and they form their opinions based on self-interest, not regard for the truth. The Pharisees condemn the crowd's ignorance of the law, but Nicodemus points out that they themselves disregard the law in their judgment of Jesus.

Pray as you are led for yourself and others.

"Lord, I can be swept into confusion by all the arguments of my own day. My knowledge is partial, my prejudices hold sway, and I am distracted from having a pure encounter with you. Let me know you and worship you with all my heart . . ." (Continue in your own words.)

Listen to Jesus.

My beloved servant, I give you my heart as you have given me yours. By faith you see me, by love you know me. What else do you ask of me today? What else is Jesus saying to you?

Ask God to show you how to live today.

"Thank you for your wonderful love for me, Lord. Let nothing ever come between us. I humbly ask that I may radiate your love to others today. Amen."

FIFTH WEEK OF LENT

In order to understand the Mystery of the Cross, it is necessary to know ahead of time that the One who suffers and who is glorified is not only a man but is the Son of God who, with his love faithful to the end, saved us.

Pope Francis
February 25, 2018

Sunday, April 7, 2019
Fifth Sunday of Lent

Know that God is present with you and ready to converse.

"Jesus, teach me just judgment by your Word."

Read the gospel: John 8:1–11.

Jesus went to the Mount of Olives. Early in the morning he came again to the temple. All the people came to him and he sat down and began to teach them. The scribes and the Pharisees brought a woman who had been caught in adultery; and making her stand before all of them, they said to him, "Teacher, this woman was caught in the very act of committing adultery. Now in the law Moses commanded us to stone such women. Now what do you say?" They said this to test him, so that they might have some charge to bring against him. Jesus bent down and wrote with his finger on the ground. When they kept on questioning him, he straightened up and said to them, "Let anyone among you who is without sin be the first to throw a stone at her." And once again he bent down and wrote on the ground. When they heard it, they went away, one by one, beginning with the elders; and Jesus was left alone with the woman standing before him. Jesus straightened up and said to her, "Woman, where are they? Has no one condemned you?" She said, "No one, sir." And Jesus said, "Neither do I condemn you. Go your way, and from now on do not sin again."

Notice what you think and feel as you read the gospel.

When the scribes and Pharisees bring a woman caught in adultery to Jesus, he teaches them mercy and shows their own sinfulness. In obedience to the law of Moses, they would stone her, but Jesus reminds them they are all sinners. Then Jesus forgives the woman and exhorts her to sin no more.

Pray as you are led for yourself and others.

"Lord, you have fulfilled the law of Moses with plentiful love and mercy. Thank you. Let me love and forgive someone I have been judging . . ." (Continue in your own words.)

Listen to Jesus.

I am glad for your sake that you see that practicing love and mercy are the ways to please God and grow in holiness. You will find happiness in this way. Walk close to me. What else is Jesus saying to you?

Ask God to show you how to live today.

"I resolve to walk with you today, Lord. Use me as you will. I want to serve and please you, but I cannot unless you work through me. Amen."

Monday, April 8, 2019

Know that God is present with you and ready to converse.

"Lord, write on my heart your laws of love. I thank you for your presence here now."

Read the gospel: John 8:12–20.

Again Jesus spoke to them, saying, "I am the light of the world. Whoever follows me will never walk in darkness but will have the light of life." Then the Pharisees said to him, "You are testifying on your own behalf; your testimony is not valid." Jesus answered, "Even if I testify on my own behalf, my testimony is valid because I know where I have come from and where I am going, but you do not know where I come from or where I am going. You judge by human standards; I judge no one. Yet even if I do judge, my judgment is valid; for it is not I alone who judge, but I and the Father who sent me. In your law it is written that the testimony of two witnesses is valid. I testify on my own behalf, and the Father who sent me testifies on my behalf." Then they said to him, "Where is your Father?" Jesus answered, "You know neither me nor my Father. If you knew me, you would know my Father also." He spoke these words while he was teaching in the treasury of the temple, but no one arrested him, because his hour had not yet come.

Notice what you think and feel as you read the gospel.

While the Pharisees are scrupulous in adhering to the Law of Moses, Jesus encourages them to look to the greater law that comes from God, the Father.

Pray as you are led for yourself and others.

"Lord, my heart is quick to judge others who do not follow the letter of the law. By your Spirit, let me seek your forgiveness and let me value obedience to those who honor your higher law . . ." (Continue in your own words.)

Listen to Jesus.

Beloved, you are right to seek holiness by my Spirit, for only in God is it possible to achieve true obedience. What else is Jesus saying to you?

Ask God to show you how to live today.

"Open my eyes and mind that I may see how I can be judgmental. Lord, show me how to put my judgments far from me, case by case. All praise to you, Lord Jesus Christ. Amen."

Tuesday, April 9, 2019

Know that God is present with you and ready to converse.

"Master of the Universe, Holy Trinity, One God, I cannot take you in. Take me into yourself. Capture me by your Word."

Read the gospel: John 8:21–30.

Again Jesus said to them, "I am going away, and you will search for me, but you will die in your sin. Where I am going, you cannot come." Then the Jews said, "Is he going to kill himself? Is that what he means by saying, 'Where I am going, you cannot come'?" He said to them, "You are from below, I am from above; you are of this world, I am not of this world. I told you that you would die in your sins, for you will die in your sins unless you believe that I am he." They said to him, "Who are you?" Jesus said to them, "Why do I speak to you at all? I have much to say about you and much to condemn; but the one who sent me is true, and I declare to the world what I have heard from him." They did not understand that he was speaking to them about the Father. So Jesus said, "When you have lifted up the Son of Man, then you will realize that I am he, and that I do nothing on my own, but I speak these things as the Father instructed me. And the one who sent me is with me; he has not left me alone, for I always do what is pleasing to him." As he was saying these things, many believed in him.

Notice what you think and feel as you read the gospel.

Jesus is thinking of his Passion, Death, Resurrection, and Ascension. He exhorts his listeners to believe in him lest they die in their sins. He tells them they will realize who he is when they lift him up on the Cross.

Pray as you are led for yourself and others.

"Lord, I know I am of this world, full of human weakness. Let me believe and come to you. I pray for all those who resist you . . ." (Continue in your own words.)

Listen to Jesus.

Your faithfulness to me touches me, dear friend. You want others to know your peace in knowing me. Our prayers for them have power with our Father. Thank you for praying with me. What else is Jesus saying to you?

Ask God to show you how to live today.

"I offer you all my thoughts, words, deeds, joys, and sorrows this day, that you may count them as a prayer for those you have given me. Keep my mind stayed on you. Amen."

Wednesday, April 10, 2019

Know that God is present with you and ready to converse.

"Jesus, give me your Spirit to know your truth and freedom."

Read the gospel: John 8:31–38 (Jn 8:31–42).

Then Jesus said to the Jews who had believed in him, "If you continue in my word, you are truly my disciples; and you will know the truth, and the truth will make you free." They answered him, "We are descendants of Abraham and have never been slaves to anyone. What do you mean by saying, 'You will be made free'?"

Jesus answered them, "Very truly, I tell you, everyone who commits sin is a slave to sin. The slave does not have a permanent place in the household; the son has a place there forever. So if the Son makes you free, you will be free indeed. I know that you are descendants of Abraham; yet you look for an opportunity to kill me, because there is no place in you for my word. I declare what I have seen in the Father's presence; as for you, you should do what you have heard from the Father."

Notice what you think and feel as you read the gospel.

Jesus declares the truth of his Word: it will make us free from sin, which will allow us to love God the Father.

Pray as you are led for yourself and others.

"Jesus, let me use the freedom you give me to avoid sin. Let me love God and desire to please God in all things. I wish to help others to see the truth of your Word and Person, Jesus . . ." (Continue in your own words.)

Listen to Jesus.

Examine your life, beloved disciple, in the light of my Word and the freedom it gives you. As you give yourself to me, turning from sin, you will rejoice in the love of God. What else is Jesus saying to you?

Ask God to show you how to live today.

"How am I free, Lord? Make me aware of moments of freedom in this day so that I may choose goodness, truth, love, and God. Amen."

Thursday, April 11, 2019

Know that God is present with you and ready to converse.

"You are here with me now, Jesus. You are always with me. Let me know you in your Word and carry you forth into my day by your Spirit."

Read the gospel: John 8:51–59.

Jesus said, "Very truly, I tell you, whoever keeps my word will never see death." The Jews said to him, "Now we know that you have a demon. Abraham died, and so did the prophets; yet you say, 'Whoever keeps my word will never taste death.' Are you greater than our father Abraham, who died? The prophets also died. Who do you claim to be?" Jesus answered, "If I glorify myself, my glory is nothing. It is my Father who glorifies me, he of whom you say, 'He is our God,' though you do not know him. But I know him; if I were to say that I do not know him, I would be a liar like you. But I do know him and I keep his word. Your ancestor Abraham rejoiced that he would see my day; he saw it and was glad." Then the Jews said to him, "You are not yet fifty years old, and have you seen Abraham?" Jesus said to them, "Very truly, I tell you, before Abraham was, I am." So they picked up stones to throw at him, but Jesus hid himself and went out of the temple.

Notice what you think and feel as you read the gospel.

The Jews scorn Jesus' claims of a special relationship with God and his ability to confer eternal life on those who keep his Word. Jesus knows they will turn on him for what seems blasphemy to them, but he is compelled to tell the truth about himself.

Pray as you are led for yourself and others.

"Word of the Father, Light of the World, grant me your Life, your Truth, your Way. I glorify you for your goodness and your generous grace to me and mine . . ." (Continue in your own words.)

Listen to Jesus.

My Father glorified my suffering. I obeyed God for love because God's purposes are all love. Let love operate in your life, child, and God will glorify your suffering as well. What else is Jesus saying to you?

Ask God to show you how to live today.

"I do suffer, Lord, in small and great ways as the days pass. I offer this suffering to our Father for love of those you have given me. Let me love as you do, Jesus. Amen."

Friday, April 12, 2019

Know that God is present with you and ready to converse.

"Jesus, Son of the Father and One with the Father in the unity of the Holy Spirit, lift me to God by your Word."

Read the gospel: John 10:31–39 (Jn 10:31–42).

The Jews took up stones again to stone him. Jesus replied, "I have shown you many good works from the Father. For which of these are you going to stone me?" The Jews answered, "It is not for a good work that we are going to stone you, but for blasphemy, because you, though only a human being, are making yourself God." Jesus answered, "Is it not written in your law, 'I said, you are gods'? If those to whom the word of God came were called 'gods'—and the scripture cannot be annulled— can you say that the one whom the Father has sanctified and sent into the world is blaspheming because I said, 'I am God's Son'? If I am not doing the works of my Father, then do not believe me. But if I do them, even though you do not believe me, believe the works, so that you may know and understand that the Father is in me and I am in the Father." Then they tried to arrest him again, but he escaped from their hands.

Notice what you think and feel as you read the gospel.

Jesus faces stoning by the many who cannot abide the notion that he is God's Son. Jesus appeals to scripture and then to his own mighty works as reasons to believe in him. He affirms again that the Father is in him and he is in the Father. He escapes arrest.

Pray as you are led for yourself and others.

"Lord, what is the difference between those who believe your Word and those who don't? I believe. Help my unbelief. I pray for those who do not believe or who suffer from doubts . . ." (Continue in your own words.)

Listen to Jesus.

Your faith is my gift to you, beloved disciple. Treasure it. Put it to use in your prayers and in your actions. Let it grow and bear fruit. What else is Jesus saying to you?

Ask God to show you how to live today.

"Lord, today when I find myself in a situation in which I may show my faith, let me do so. Let me remember your words and walk in the faith you have given me. Amen."

Saturday, April 13, 2019

Know that God is present with you and ready to converse.

"I am looking for you, Jesus, and ask you to let me find you, know you, and love you in your Word. Speak to me, Lord."

Read the gospel: John 11:45–53 (Jn 11:45–56).

Many of the Jews therefore, who had come with Mary and had seen what Jesus did, believed in him. But some of them went to the Pharisees and told them what he had done. So the chief priests and the Pharisees called a meeting of the council, and said, "What are we to do? This man is performing many signs. If we let him go on like this, everyone will believe in him, and the Romans will come and destroy both our holy place and our nation." But one of them, Caiaphas, who was high priest that year, said to them, "You know nothing at all! You do not understand that it is better for you to have one man die for the people than to have the whole nation destroyed." He did not say this on his own, but being high priest that year he prophesied that Jesus was about to die for the nation, and not for the nation only, but to gather into one the dispersed children of God. So from that day on they planned to put him to death.

Notice what you think and feel as you read the gospel.

Feeling threatened by Jesus' power and growing influence, the Pharisees call a meeting. The chief priest, Caiaphas, suggests that Jesus may make a good scapegoat for the Jewish people; his comment is truer than he realized at the time.

Pray as you are led for yourself and others.

"Jesus, when you hide yourself and show yourself, you are acting in obedience to God, not out of fear of others. Let me be as you were, led only by the will of God. Give me grace to do God's will . . ." (Continue in your own words.)

Listen to Jesus.

Servant of God, I come to you with love this moment, and I will be close to you all day. As you give yourself to God, God's will is done. Follow me. What else is Jesus saying to you?

Ask God to show you how to live today.

"Jesus, you came to earth and changed history. Work with me in my life to change things, that I may hasten the coming of the kingdom of God. Thank you. Amen."

HOLY WEEK

We know that the state of sin distances us from God. But in fact, sin is the way that we distance ourselves from him. Yet that does not mean that God distances himself from us. The state of weakness and confusion that results from sin is one more reason for God to remain close to us. The certainty of this should accompany us throughout our lives. . . . His grace is constantly at work in us, to strengthen our hope that his love will never be lacking, in spite of any sin we may have committed by rejecting his presence in our lives.

Pope Francis
March 9, 2018

Sunday, April 14, 2019
Palm Sunday of the Lord's Passion

Know that God is present with you and ready to converse.

"Jesus, you are preparing to give yourself to me. Show me how to receive you."

Read the gospel: Luke 22:14–23 (Lk 22:14–23:56).

When the hour came, Jesus took his place at the table, and the apostles with him. He said to them, "I have eagerly desired to eat this Passover with you before I suffer; for I tell you, I will not eat it until it is fulfilled in the kingdom of God." Then he took a cup, and after giving thanks he said, "Take this and divide it among yourselves; for I tell you that from now on I will not drink of the fruit of the vine until the kingdom of God comes." Then he took a loaf of bread, and when he had given thanks, he broke it and gave it to them, saying, "This is my body, which is given for you. Do this in remembrance of me." And he did the same with the cup after supper, saying, "This cup that is poured out for you is the new covenant in my blood. But see, the one who betrays me is with me, and his hand is on the table. For the Son of Man is going as it has been determined, but woe to that one by whom he is betrayed!" Then they began to ask one another which one of them it could be who would do this.

Notice what you think and feel as you read the gospel.

The Passover supper with the Twelve serves as the foundation of the Eucharistic rites we celebrate today. The bread Jesus offers at the Passover supper is his Body; the wine his Blood. We are to receive the bread and wine of the Eucharist in the same faith his disciples did.

Pray as you are led for yourself and others.

"Lord, I do not want to betray you as Judas did or even to deny you as Peter did after you were arrested. I want to come to you and receive you with perfect faith. Let your Eucharist strengthen me, Lord, that I may show your love to others . . ." (Continue in your own words.)

Listen to Jesus.

You are mine, dearest beloved, and I draw you to me. Stay with me, for I have power to bestow holiness and blessing upon you. By them, you will glorify God and help others. Continue in my love. What else is Jesus saying to you?

Ask God to show you how to live today.

"God, remain with me. Let me glorify you in every thought, word, and deed today. Thank you for your Body and Blood, given to me. Amen."

Monday, April 15, 2019

Know that God is present with you and ready to converse.

"Jesus, Word of the Father, enter my heart, mind, soul, and spirit as I read and pray today."

Read the gospel: John 12:1–8 (Jn 12:1–11).

Six days before the Passover Jesus came to Bethany, the home of Lazarus, whom he had raised from the dead. There they gave a dinner for him. Martha served, and Lazarus was one of those at the table with him. Mary took a pound of costly perfume made of pure nard, anointed Jesus' feet, and wiped them with her hair. The house was filled with the fragrance of the perfume. But Judas Iscariot, one of his disciples (the one who was about to betray him), said, "Why was this perfume not sold for three hundred denarii and the money given to the poor?" (He said this not because he cared about the poor, but because he was a thief; he kept the common purse and used to steal what was put into it.) Jesus said, "Leave her alone. She bought it so that she might keep it for the day of my burial. You always have the poor with you, but you do not always have me."

Notice what you think and feel as you read the gospel.

Lazarus, who was raised from the dead, is hosting Jesus, whom Mary symbolically prepares for burial. Jesus embraces the supposed excess of Mary's act, to Judas's disapproval. Yet Jesus reminds him that honoring the Lord and caring for the poor go hand in hand.

Pray as you are led for yourself and others.

"Jesus, I, too, want to honor you, want to fall at your feet in awe and wonder and love . . ." (Continue in your own words.)

Listen to Jesus.

Dear disciple, come to me in the sacraments, honor me with true humility and openness, and love me in all your brothers and sisters. What else is Jesus saying to you?

Ask God to show you how to live today.

"Lord, allow me to glorify you through my words and actions today. Thank you. Amen."

Tuesday, April 16, 2019

Know that God is present with you and ready to converse.

"Jesus, let me know you better so that I may follow you more closely. Teach me by your Word."

Read the gospel: John 13:21–33, 36–38.

After saying this Jesus was troubled in spirit, and declared, "Very truly, I tell you, one of you will betray me." The disciples looked at one another, uncertain of whom he was speaking. One of his disciples—the one whom Jesus loved—was reclining next to him; Simon Peter therefore motioned to him to ask Jesus of whom he was speaking. So while reclining next to Jesus, he asked him, "Lord, who is it?" Jesus answered, "It is the one to whom I give this piece of bread when I have dipped it in the dish." So when he had dipped the piece of bread, he gave it to Judas son of Simon Iscariot. After he received the piece of bread, Satan entered into him. Jesus said to him, "Do quickly what you are going to do." Now no one at the table knew why he said this to him. Some thought that, because Judas had the common purse, Jesus was telling him, "Buy what we need for the festival"; or, that he should give something to the poor. So, after receiving the piece of bread, he immediately went out. And it was night.

When he had gone out, Jesus said, "Now the Son of Man has been glorified, and God has been glorified in him. If God has been glorified in him, God will also glorify him in himself and will glorify him at once. Little children, I am with you only a little longer. You will look for me; and as I said to the Jews so now I say to you, 'Where I am going, you cannot come.'" . . .

Simon Peter said to him, "Lord, where are you going?" Jesus answered, "Where I am going, you cannot follow me now; but you will follow afterwards." Peter said to him, "Lord, why can I not follow you now? I will lay down my life for you." Jesus answered, "Will you lay down your life for me? Very truly, I tell you, before the cock crows, you will have denied me three times."

Notice what you think and feel as you read the gospel.

Jesus begins the evening of the Passover troubled by his impending betrayal, but when Judas leaves to betray him, Jesus speaks of glory and his departure to a place they cannot come. Peter protests, but Jesus predicts his denial.

Pray as you are led for yourself and others.

"Lord, I have denied you, and I'm sorry. But I ask you to let me follow you, dying to myself and forsaking all for you . . ." (Continue in your own words.)

Listen to Jesus.

If I am the love of your life, if you give your whole heart to me, I will guide you in my path of service. Will you suffer? Yes. But you will also share my glory. What else is Jesus saying to you?

Ask God to show you how to live today.

"Help me to get my eyes off of myself, Lord, and look upon you, the crucified and risen King of Glory. I praise your holy name. Amen."

Wednesday, April 17, 2019

Know that God is present with you and ready to converse.

"Lord, I have been close to you, and you are with me now. Keep me from all betrayal; let me never turn away from you."

Read the gospel: Matthew 26:14–25.

Then one of the twelve, who was called Judas Iscariot, went to the chief priests and said, "What will you give me if I betray him to you?" They paid him thirty pieces of silver. And from that moment he began to look for an opportunity to betray him.

On the first day of Unleavened Bread the disciples came to Jesus, saying, "Where do you want us to make the preparations for you to eat the Passover?" He said, "Go into the city to a certain man, and say to him, 'The Teacher says, My time is near; I will keep the Passover at your house with my disciples.'" So the disciples did as Jesus had directed them, and they prepared the Passover meal.

When it was evening, he took his place with the twelve; and while they were eating, he said, "Truly I tell you, one of you will betray me." And they became greatly distressed and began to say to him one after another, "Surely not I, Lord?" He answered, "The one who has dipped his hand into the bowl with me will betray me. The Son of Man goes as it is written of him, but woe to that one by whom the Son of Man is betrayed! It would have been better for that one not to have been born." Judas, who betrayed him, said, "Surely not I, Rabbi?" He replied, "You have said so."

Notice what you think and feel as you read the gospel.

Judas, though he had traveled with Jesus, heard his preaching, seen his miracles, and was given a position of trust, agrees to betray Jesus to the chief priests for money. Judas shows that all people are subject to temptation, no matter their experiences or status.

Pray as you are led for yourself and others.

"Lord, let me never forget that I am weak, easily tempted to value things other than you. Forgive me for my weakness, love me and let me do what pleases you . . ." (Continue in your own words.)

Listen to Jesus.

I do love you, my dear child. Open yourself in all your failure and weakness to me. I understand. I will wash and heal you and make you strong. What else is Jesus saying to you?

Ask God to show you how to live today.

"I need you, Lord. Today I need you to see well, to love well, to speak well, and to do well. Thank you. Amen."

Thursday, April 18, 2019
Holy Thursday

Know that God is present with you and ready to converse.

"Jesus, Son of the Father, you show me how you live by your Word. Let your lessons be bound to my heart."

Read the gospel: John 13:2b–15 (Jn 13:1–15).

And during supper Jesus, knowing that the Father had given all things into his hands, and that he had come from God and was going to God, got up from the table, took off his outer robe, and tied a towel around himself. Then he poured water into a basin and began to wash the disciples' feet and to wipe them with the towel that was tied around him. He came to Simon Peter, who said to him, "Lord, are you going to wash my feet?" Jesus answered, "You do not know now what I am doing, but later you will understand." Peter said to him, "You will never wash my feet." Jesus answered, "Unless I wash you, you have no share with me." Simon Peter said to him, "Lord, not my feet only but also my hands and my head!" Jesus said to him, "One who has bathed does not need to wash, except for the feet, but is entirely clean. And you are clean, though not all of you." For he knew who was to betray him; for this reason he said, "Not all of you are clean."

After he had washed their feet, had put on his robe, and had returned to the table, he said to them, "Do you know what I have done to you? You call me Teacher and Lord—and you are right, for that is what I am. So if I, your Lord and Teacher, have washed your feet, you also ought to wash one another's feet. For I have set you an example, that you also should do as I have done to you."

Notice what you think and feel as you read the gospel.

Jesus teaches by example that the greatest ones will wash the feet of those they serve. Not just in the washing of the feet but throughout his ministry Jesus served others.

Pray as you are led for yourself and others.

"How shall I put your lesson into action, Lord? Help me reach the people I intend to serve, including . . ." (Continue in your own words.)

Listen to Jesus.

Find great joy in humble service, but do not glorify yourself, and you will follow my commands. What else is Jesus saying to you?

Ask God to show you how to live today.

"Give me the skill, Jesus, to serve others without embarrassing them or striking a false pose of humility. Amen."

Friday, April 19, 2019
Good Friday

Know that God is present with you and ready to converse.

"Lord, I come to you on this day with awe and trembling. You willingly went to your death for love of me."

Read the gospel: John 18:1–19:42.

After Jesus had spoken these words, he went out with his disciples across the Kidron valley to a place where there was a garden, which he and his disciples entered. Now Judas, who betrayed him, also knew the place, because Jesus often met there with his disciples. So Judas brought a detachment of soldiers together with police from the chief priests and the Pharisees, and they came there with lanterns and torches and weapons. Then Jesus, knowing all that was to happen to him, came forward and asked them, "For whom are you looking?" They answered, "Jesus of Nazareth." Jesus replied, "I am he." Judas, who betrayed him, was standing with them. When Jesus said to them, "I am he," they stepped back and fell to the ground. Again he asked them, "For whom are you looking?" And they said, "Jesus of Nazareth." Jesus answered, "I told you that I am he. So if you are looking for me, let these men go." This was to fulfill the word that he had spoken, "I did not lose a single one of those whom you gave me." Then Simon Peter, who had a sword, drew it, struck the high priest's slave, and cut off his right ear. The slave's name was Malchus. Jesus said to Peter, "Put your sword back into its sheath. Am I not to drink the cup that the Father has given me?"

So the soldiers, their officer, and the Jewish police arrested Jesus and bound him. First they took him to Annas, who was the father-in-law of Caiaphas, the high priest that year. Caiaphas was the one who had advised the Jews that it was better to have one person die for the people.

Simon Peter and another disciple followed Jesus. Since that disciple was known to the high priest, he went with Jesus into the courtyard of the high priest, but Peter was standing outside at the gate. So the other disciple, who was known to the high priest, went out, spoke to the woman who guarded the gate, and brought Peter in. The woman said to Peter, "You are not also one of this man's disciples, are you?" He said, "I am not." Now the slaves and the police had made a charcoal fire because it was cold, and they were standing round it and warming themselves. Peter also was standing with them and warming himself.

Then the high priest questioned Jesus about his disciples and about his teaching. Jesus answered, "I have spoken openly to the world; I have always taught in synagogues and in the temple, where all the Jews come together. I have said nothing in secret. Why do you ask me? Ask those who heard what I said to them; they know what I said." When he had said this, one of the police standing nearby struck Jesus on the face, saying, "Is that how you answer the high priest?" Jesus answered, "If I have spoken wrongly, testify to the wrong. But if I have spoken rightly, why do you strike me?" Then Annas sent him bound to Caiaphas the high priest.

Now Simon Peter was standing and warming himself. They asked him, "You are not also one of his disciples, are you?" He denied it and said, "I am not." One of the slaves of the high priest, a relative of the man whose ear Peter had cut off, asked, "Did I not see you in the garden with him?" Again Peter denied it, and at that moment the cock crowed.

Then they took Jesus from Caiaphas to Pilate's headquarters. It was early in the morning. They themselves did not enter the headquarters, so as to avoid ritual defilement and to be able to eat the Passover. So Pilate went out to them and said, "What accusation do you bring against this man?" They answered, "If this man were not a criminal, we would not have handed him over to you." Pilate said to them, "Take him yourselves and judge him according to your law." The Jews replied, "We are not permitted to put anyone to death." (This was to fulfill what Jesus had said when he indicated the kind of death he was to die.)

Then Pilate entered the headquarters again, summoned Jesus, and asked him, "Are you the King of the Jews?" Jesus answered, "Do you ask this on your own, or did others tell you about me?" Pilate replied, "I am not a Jew, am I? Your own nation and the chief priests have handed you over to me. What have you done?" Jesus answered, "My kingdom is not from this world. If my kingdom were from this world, my followers would be fighting to keep me from being handed over to the Jews. But as it is, my kingdom is not from here." Pilate asked him, "So you are a king?" Jesus answered,

"You say that I am a king. For this I was born, and for this I came into the world, to testify to the truth. Everyone who belongs to the truth listens to my voice." Pilate asked him, "What is truth?"

After he had said this, he went out to the Jews again and told them, "I find no case against him. But you have a custom that I release someone for you at the Passover. Do you want me to release for you the King of the Jews?" They shouted in reply, "Not this man, but Barabbas!" Now Barabbas was a bandit.

Then Pilate took Jesus and had him flogged. And the soldiers wove a crown of thorns and put it on his head, and they dressed him in a purple robe. They kept coming up to him, saying, "Hail, King of the Jews!" and striking him on the face. Pilate went out again and said to them, "Look, I am bringing him out to you to let you know that I find no case against him." So Jesus came out, wearing the crown of thorns and the purple robe. Pilate said to them, "Here is the man!" When the chief priests and the police saw him, they shouted, "Crucify him! Crucify him!" Pilate said to them, "Take him yourselves and crucify him; I find no case against him." The Jews answered him, "We have a law, and according to that law he ought to die because he has claimed to be the Son of God."

Now when Pilate heard this, he was more afraid than ever. He entered his headquarters again and asked Jesus, "Where are you from?" But Jesus gave him no answer. Pilate therefore said to him, "Do you refuse to speak to me? Do you not know that I have power to release you, and power to crucify you?" Jesus answered him, "You would have no power over me unless it had been given you from above; therefore the one who handed me over to you is guilty of a greater sin." From then on Pilate tried to release him, but the Jews cried out, "If you release this man, you are no friend of the emperor. Everyone who claims to be a king sets himself against the emperor."

When Pilate heard these words, he brought Jesus outside and sat on the judge's bench at a place called The Stone Pavement, or in Hebrew Gabbatha. Now it was the day of Preparation for the Passover; and it was about noon. He said to the Jews, "Here is your King!" They cried out, "Away with him! Away with him! Crucify him!" Pilate asked them, "Shall I crucify your King?" The chief priests answered, "We have no king but the emperor." Then he handed him over to them to be crucified.

So they took Jesus; and carrying the cross by himself, he went out to what is called The Place of the Skull, which in Hebrew is called Golgotha. There they crucified him, and with him two others, one on either side, with Jesus between them. Pilate also had an inscription written and put on the cross. It read, "Jesus of Nazareth, the King of the Jews." Many of the Jews read this inscription, because the place where Jesus was crucified was near the city; and it was written in Hebrew, in Latin, and in Greek. Then the chief priests of the Jews said to Pilate, "Do not write, 'The King of the Jews,' but, 'This man said, I am King of the Jews.'" Pilate answered, "What I have written I have written." When the soldiers had crucified Jesus, they took his clothes and divided them into four parts, one for each soldier. They also took his tunic; now the tunic was seamless, woven in one piece from the top. So they said to one another, "Let us not tear it, but cast lots for it to see who will get it." This was to fulfill what the scripture says,

"They divided my clothes among themselves,
   and for my clothing they cast lots."

And that is what the soldiers did.

Meanwhile, standing near the cross of Jesus were his mother, and his mother's sister, Mary the wife of Clopas, and Mary Magdalene. When Jesus saw his mother and the disciple whom he loved standing beside her, he said to his mother, "Woman, here is your son." Then he said to the disciple, "Here is your mother." And from that hour the disciple took her into his own home.

After this, when Jesus knew that all was now finished, he said (in order to fulfill the scripture), "I am thirsty." A jar full of sour wine was standing there. So they put a sponge full of the wine on a branch of hyssop and held it to his mouth. When Jesus had received the wine, he said, "It is finished." Then he bowed his head and gave up his spirit.

Since it was the day of Preparation, the Jews did not want the bodies left on the cross during the sabbath, especially because that sabbath was a day of great solemnity. So they asked Pilate to have the legs of the crucified men broken and the bodies removed. Then the soldiers came and broke the legs of the first and of the other who had been crucified with him. But when they came to Jesus and saw that he was already dead, they did not break his legs. Instead, one of the soldiers pierced his side with a spear, and at once blood and water came out. (He who saw this has testified so that you also may believe. His testimony is true, and he knows that he tells the truth.) These things occurred so that the scripture might be fulfilled, "None of his bones shall be broken." And again another passage of scripture says, "They will look on the one whom they have pierced."

After these things, Joseph of Arimathea, who was a disciple of Jesus, though a secret one because of his fear of the Jews, asked Pilate to let him take away the body of Jesus. Pilate gave him permission; so he came and removed his body. Nicodemus, who had at first come to Jesus by night, also came, bringing a mixture of myrrh and aloes, weighing about a hundred pounds. They took the body of Jesus and wrapped it with the spices in linen cloths, according to the burial custom of the Jews. Now there was a garden in the place where he was crucified, and in the garden there was a new tomb in which no one had ever been laid. And so, because it was the Jewish day of Preparation, and the tomb was nearby, they laid Jesus there.

Notice what you think and feel as you read the gospel.

How brave Jesus was throughout that horrible ordeal, his betrayal, torture, and death! In the end, blood and water flowed out of his pierced side, emblematic of our entering into redemption through the blood of his sacrifice and in Baptism by his Church.

Pray as you are led for yourself and others.

"Jesus, I am not worthy, but you died for love of me. Let me be washed clean of all sin by your blood. Let me thank you and glorify you this moment . . ." (Continue in your own words.)

Listen to Jesus.

My child, I love you now as I loved you then. Do you love me? What else is Jesus saying to you?

Ask God to show you how to live today.

"Lord, I am burdened and broken by my own crosses, even today. Give me your courage and your heart to journey today until the end. Amen."

Saturday, April 20, 2019
Holy Saturday

Know that God is present with you and ready to converse.

"Jesus, you live. Live in me and guide me by your Word."

Read the gospel: Luke 24:1–12.

But on the first day of the week, at early dawn, the women came to the tomb, taking the spices that they had prepared. They found the stone rolled away from the tomb, but when they went in, they did not find the body. While they were perplexed about this, suddenly two men in dazzling clothes stood beside them. The women were terrified and bowed their faces to the ground, but the men said to them, "Why do you look for the living among the dead? He is not here, but has risen. Remember how he told you, while he was still in Galilee, that the Son of Man must be handed over to sinners, and be crucified, and on the third day rise again." Then they remembered his words, and returning from the tomb, they told all this to the eleven and to all the rest. Now it was Mary Magdalene, Joanna, Mary the mother of James, and the other women with them who told this to the apostles. But these words seemed to them an idle tale, and they did not believe them. But Peter got up and ran to the tomb; stooping and looking in, he saw the linen cloths by themselves; then he went home, amazed at what had happened.

Notice what you think and feel as you read the gospel.

The women are the first to know and believe Jesus is alive. They understood. They worshiped. They obeyed.

Pray as you are led for yourself and others.

"Lord, strengthen my faith in the miracle of your Resurrection. Let it be so real to me that the living Jesus becomes the center of my life. Let others see you through me . . ." (Continue in your own words.)

Listen to Jesus.

I take care of you, beloved. Trust in me. Let others know you do. Ask me for whatever you need. What else is Jesus saying to you?

Ask God to show you how to live today.

"Show me how to recognize you, worship you, and obey you today. I need you, Lord. Amen."

Sunday, April 21, 2019
Easter Sunday

Know that God is present with you and ready to converse.

"Risen Lord, you have revealed yourself to many. Reveal yourself to me."

Read the gospel: Luke 24:13–35.

Now on that same day two of them were going to a village called Emmaus, about seven miles from Jerusalem, and talking with each other about all these things that had happened. While they were talking and discussing, Jesus himself came near and went with them, but their eyes were kept from recognizing him. And he said to them, "What are you discussing with each other while you walk along?" They stood still, looking sad. Then one of them, whose name was Cleopas, answered him, "Are you the only stranger in Jerusalem who does not know the things that have taken place there in these days?" He asked them, "What things?" They replied, "The things about Jesus of Nazareth, who was a prophet mighty in deed and word before God and all the people, and how our chief priests and leaders handed him over to be condemned to death and crucified him. But we had hoped that he was the one to redeem Israel. Yes, and besides all this, it is now the third day since these things took place. Moreover, some women of our group astounded us. They were at the tomb early this morning, and when they did not find his body there, they came back and told us that they had indeed seen a vision of angels who said that he was alive. Some of those who were with us went to the tomb and found it just as the women had said; but they did not see him." Then he said to them, "Oh, how foolish you are, and how slow of heart to believe all that the prophets have declared! Was it not necessary that the Messiah should suffer these things and then enter into his glory?" Then beginning with Moses and all the prophets, he interpreted to them the things about himself in all the scriptures.

As they came near the village to which they were going, he walked ahead as if he were going on. But they urged him strongly, saying, "Stay with us, because it is almost evening and the day is now nearly over." So he went in to stay with them. When he was at the table with them, he took bread, blessed and broke it, and gave it to them. Then their eyes were opened, and they recognized him; and he vanished from their sight. They said to each other, "Were not our hearts burning within us while he was talking to us on the road, while he was opening the scriptures to us?" That same hour they got up and returned to Jerusalem; and they found the eleven and their companions gathered together. They were saying, "The Lord has risen indeed, and he has appeared to Simon!" Then they told what had happened on the road, and how he had been made known to them in the breaking of the bread.

Notice what you think and feel as you read the gospel.

Why are the disciples in this story going to Emmaus? Perhaps they're confused, disheartened, scared, so they're going home. Jesus comes to them, though they don't recognize it's him; he walks alongside them, explains things to them. His words give them comfort, and they ask him to stay with them. And when he breaks the bread and feeds them, suddenly they see him—everything is made clear and bright. In his words he has given them courage, and in the bread he has given them strength, and they jump up that moment and run back to Jerusalem, back to the ministry to which Jesus calls all Christians.

Pray as you are led for yourself and others.

"The world has never seen such a miracle as your Resurrection, Lord. Alleluia! Fill me with knowledge of you, sustain me, that I may hurry to do your will . . ." (Continue in your own words.)

Listen to Jesus.

I will walk alongside you, dear one. With me you will do well, and those around you will notice. What else is Jesus saying to you?

Ask God to show you how to live today.

"I would like to help others believe in you, Lord. Let me see the opportunities to say and do things that reveal you. You are one with Almighty God, Father, Son, and Holy Spirit. Amen."

The Pope's Worldwide Prayer Network is an international ecclesial ministry served by the Jesuits that reaches more than 50 million participants worldwide through its popular website, talks, conferences, radio outreach, publications, and retreats. Each year the Holy Father asks that Christians and non-Christians alike join in praying for his particular intentions on the challenges facing humanity. The regional US–Canadian office can be found at popesprayerusa.net and popesprayercanada.net.